Diaries of a Man Who Believes in Angels

Ged Thompson

Best Wishes
Ged

Published by Angelus Poetry
angeluspoetry@yahoo.com

ISBN 978-0-9934737-3-9

Cover artwork and illustrations
by Holly Fowler

Printed by Imprint Digital
Upton Pyne, Exeter, Devon
imprintdigital.com

Dedicated to the memory of
Spike

Contents

Introduction by Ryan Leahey *7*
Preface *11*
Sorry I forgot *13*

[01/03/17] Ticking tin of beans 17
[21/03/17] You stop dying slowly 18
[28/03/17] Buddy & the psychologist 20
[27/04/17] Stan & Mary 23
[05/05/17] Mr Willis 26
[16/05/17] Flame & biscuit 30
[11/06/17] Sweet shop Saṃsāra 33
[13/06/17] A year of tears & a taxi 34
[18/06/17] Dickhead blocker 39
[19/06/17] Sir cares 42
[20/06/17] Bad Buddy lives 43
[05/07/17] Star sailing 44
[07/07/17] Mrs S 46
[10/07/17] Trainspotting 2 48
[12/07/17] Sentimental psychometry 50
[15/07/17] Fucked-up world 51
[18/07/17] Aeroplanes & ripped kimonos 52
[30/07/17] The bride who did not smile 55

[20/08/17] Albie's story 59
[26/08/17] Shithouse culture 63
[12/09/17] Ice skaters & hugs 66
[16/09/17] Shields & pride 68
[17/09/17] The Stockies 71
[07/10/17] The devil & a dead cockatoo 76
[08/10/17] Fish Finger Head 79
[09/10/17] Chair catchers 85
[25/10/17] Black dogs & Bruce Springsteen ... 86
[18/11/17] Don't fear the Reaper 89
[20/11/17] Finding home in Knoydart 90
[29/11/17] Last breaths 92
[11/12/17] When a leaf becomes a leave 93

Just one more thing… *96*

[22/10/16] On his own two feet 97

Acknowledgements *102*
About the Author *103*
Also from this Author *104*
Workshops Available *104*

Introduction

I first met Ged Thompson in around 2013 on Lark Lane, the long-standing bohemian heartbeat of Liverpool. I recall seeing him perform for the first time, and being overawed by his effortless delivery and the pregnant pauses that punctuated his poetry. I remember thinking that, for the first time at that particular venue, here was a Liverpool poet that had the grit, honesty and confidence to not only write some of the most incredibly beautiful and thought-provoking poetry that I had ever witnessed, but also to convey it; less a poet reciting a verse, more an actor living out a production, and seemingly one which mirrored his own distinctly scouse upbringing. In particular, I recall hearing his poem 'The Coin Purloin' for the first time, and being dumbstruck for several seconds as it permeated whatever coat of alcohol I had donned that particular night. As it happens, that one still gets me right in the feels. But I digress.

I had performed at the gig there myself, from time to time, and I liked to think that my poetry was half-decent; people seemed to respond with primarily positive feedback, and often we – that is, the organisers, the poets, comedians, singers, musicians, and half of the audience – would end up finishing the night with a bottle or four of red wine in Keith's Wine Bar. For those who have never had the pleasure of visiting Lark Lane, Keith's is a staple venue for artists, writers and other creative souls, and has been since 1968. Until last year, I'm fairly sure that the décor hadn't changed since it was built, a sort of crumbling, mustard-coloured palace of debauchery.

That night, I recall the usual routine of settling down to wine and witticisms around one of the old, almost medieval benches, when Ged arrived and joined the group. Still reeling from the poetic uppercut he had delivered to me an hour or so earlier, I didn't speak to him directly that night. I felt I couldn't risk being labelled a poet; the fear of being put on the spot and potentially having to reel off something ad hoc was too great. However, it wasn't long until the shoe was on the other foot and, after one gruelling gig with a particularly critical and vocally displeased audience (who, no doubt, had been expecting someone more professional – a real poet, perhaps), I left the stage with my heart (and my stomach) in my cherry red Dr Martens. As I meandered to the bar, trying not to catch the eye of the guy who had loudly declared that I was 'shit' on the way, I instead stumbled into Ged who was sitting nearby with a friend. This time, he stood up and shook my hand, patted me on the back, and told me how much he had loved the honesty in my poetry and the conviction with which I had delivered it. He was so complimentary (and coming from someone who I respected so much) that I was initially taken aback. I left the conversation elated, the sour taste of my disappointing and shaky performance dissipating as I continued on my quest for alcohol.

That night, I saw him perform for the second time, and I watched that same room fall silent as he delivered his repertoire. I watched him dwell on every word, every weighted pause lingering like smoke in some forgotten, downtown jazz bar; his customary half-smirk playing on his lips as he skilfully conducted the audience, bubbling laughter erupting into a crescendo of applause. This was poetry from the heart; poetry that snuck up behind the accepted rules of the craft and kicked its doors in. This was a different class – and it was working.

Months later, Ged and I had met a few more times, usually at one venue or another, and I like to think that we had become friends through a shared bond of poetry and, perhaps, some shared experiences in other aspects of life. I had ceased writing as often as I had previously, whereas Ged seemed to be gaining traction within the local scene and gaining confidence. He told me that he was writing a book about fairies, trolls and magic; that it would be a children's book based on the tales that he regularly told his own Son, Buddy, whom it would ultimately be dedicated to. At the time, I didn't take him very seriously; writers, after all, have a habit of meandering into fantasy at a moment's notice, and how many times have I, myself, stated confidently (after several glasses of amber liquid) that I was finally going to start writing my novel. Tomorrow.

So, it perhaps came as a surprise (though, knowing Ged as I do now, it shouldn't have done) when he produced his first book – the wonderful, ethereal *Middle Earth Magic* – and asked me what I thought. As I flicked through, I could tell immediately that it was something special; nothing less than I would have expected from Ged (although, perhaps, with less crime, sex, and swearing than his previous material). I went to the very first book reading at Write Blend, a fabulous little coffee shop in Waterloo, where a visibly nervous – but nonetheless whimsical – Ged delivered yet another electric performance. Prior to leaving, I asked him to sign my freshly-purchased copy, and he obliged gleefully, beaming as he wrote. As I left for the night, I opened the back cover and saw what he had written – "To Ryan, one of my favourite poets, love Ged".

Not long after that, I moved away from my idyll near Sefton Park and out to the relative grey of North Liverpool, where I stopped attending the poetry gigs and visits to Keith's became an increasingly rare treat. I tried my best to keep in touch with Ged via social media – such is the modern way – and every so often I would read snippets of his new material and send him some of my own. I like to think that I became somewhat of a sounding board – a role I took seriously, and still do. Then, a few months ago, Ged mentioned that he had begun working on a new project and asked if I could have a look at it, once it was completed, and give my verdict. He would go on to hand me a manuscript entitled *Diaries of a Man Who Believes in Angels;* the first copy of the book that you hold in your hand as you read this introduction.

So, I read, and as I did so, I felt that same, familiar feeling that I had felt the first time I heard Ged perform his poetry live. Unlike *Middle Earth Magic,* these are not the slick, smooth fairytales that went delving in the mystical woods for fairies and elves; these are tales of hope, sadness, love; of loss, pain, joy, faith, grit, childhood, and occasional violence – tales that don't so much peer out into the world beyond the pages, but rather look in at the people within them. It is written in diary format, which gives it a sense of the passing of time; and as you read through the pages, it feels like a journey from one place to another. It speaks of the world, from the 'Shithouses' and 'Stockies' that raised the author, to the journey that he takes with his partner-in-crime (the irrepressible Mrs S), dancing gracefully towards what lies beyond this realm and cheerfully into the next. What stood out, for me, were the underlying themes that ran beneath the otherwise unrelated tales; that we are all on a journey, and that despite the setbacks and occasional disasters that happen on our way up the mountain, that ultimately we survive because of friends and family. And because, even in our darkest hour, there is always someone willing to lend us their shield.

I hope you enjoy reading *Diaries of a Man Who Believes in Angels* as much as I did. Another beautiful journey into the mind of the ever-brilliant Ged Thompson.

Ryan Leahey

Preface

As I sit here at home weaving the final entries of this book together, many thoughts cross my mind. This morning I took a picture of the printed manuscript that sits on the table before me and sent it to my dear friend in Spain, to let her know that the idea was finally manifesting into a reality. My friend asked me if I was proud of myself and I told her that I was proud of the honesty within the entries, and admitted that I have wobbled on a number of occasions as to whether or not they may be too personal to put out into the public domain. I told her how I have had to keep reminding myself of how important it is for everyone, not just oneself, to tell our stories. After all, there is not much that one human can think or feel that others have not also thought or felt to a greater or lesser degree. We all have our stories and, in the end, they may be all that we are to become. I'm a collector of tales, not just of my own but also of other people's. Hearing other people's stories lets us know that we are not alone in hopes, fears and a search for magic in the mundane. Writing for me, is as much a coping mechanism as an art form, and in these open diary extracts that is what I am trying to do; just cope. Life moves so quickly and we live so unnaturally in modern culture that at times the lens that I view the world through becomes fogged and out of focus. It is often hard to remember what is important and what is not. Sometimes the small things seem huge, the huge things seem small, and we are left in the middle feeling like nothing at all. The keeping of a diary helps me to refocus, realign, and clearly identify with the one fundamental truth that distinguishes angels from demons and philanthropists from misanthropes. The truth that; love is enormous and everything else is tiny. It is our redemption, salvation and emancipation from darkness; a light that passes beyond life, death, time and space.

It is all that we have forgotten and all that we have left to remember.

Ged Thompson

Sorry I Forgot

I'm sorry I'm late, and I'm sorry I've been absent. I just totally forgot, you see; forgot who I was. I was in a dream where I was an electrician, and every day I got up, got into a van, and drove it to a building site. Then, people there bought chunks of my life from me with pieces of paper; paper that had pictures on, pictures of a woman that I've never even met. I swapped the pictures of the woman for some stuff that didn't really matter and then, the next morning, I got into the van again to collect more. It wasn't a bad dream, but it was all in grey. You see, this morning, I woke up and my room looked different. I could see colours again, and this time I didn't get in the van; I went to the place where I run. Only I didn't run; I walked. I smelled the trees, heard the drum-beat of raindrops falling upon their leaves, and it felt as though my heart started to beat again. A feather fell and a voice whispered to me *"You're a writer"* and I smiled and said sorry for dreaming the wrong dream, sorry that I forgot.

"I am a feather for each wind that blows."

William Shakespeare

Ticking tin of beans *1st March 2017*

This week has been a wee bit of a train wreck (long story, I'll leave that there). Then this afternoon I was doing some story-telling in a primary school in Bootle, and I've got all these little eyes looking up at me. I start telling them about leprechauns and monsters in castles, as I do like, and it goes all quiet; all these brilliant, unclouded little minds feeding off poetry and stories about magic. Then, as I'm wrapping up the session, I look down at this one young boy seated on the floor of the assembly hall, his arm sticking up straight to the sky like a rocket ship about to take off. He had that expression on his face that only a child could have; when words want to burst out of their head like a ticking tin of beans begging to explode on a bonfire. I just looked at him and asked "Yes mate?" and he replied "Sir, you're amazing!", and then beamed out this huge smile. The type of smile that makes you momentarily forget a bad week, like a beam of sunlight vanquishes a vampire. I got a little choked-up, in a good way.

Then, as I was driving home, I finally realised what I wanted to be when I grow up. I want to work with children.

You stop dying slowly *21st March 2017*

Something nice happened...

I was doing some poetry stuff with a group of sixth formers on the Wirral a couple of weeks ago. I have to say 'stuff' because I'm not sure what I'm going to do until after I've done it, and not sure what I'm going to say until after I've said it. I don't really have a set lesson plan as such – my workshop technique is what I'd describe as 'intuitive winging'. We covered a few things; I gave my thoughts on how poetry can evoke emotional resonance, ease internal tensions of opposites, how I believe that most poetry is a letter from higher-self engaging a call to arms from lower-self. Then I threw the floor open to discussion, let them cognitively meander with no set destination, with no right or wrong answers. One pupil quoted Cartesian Philosophy, even remembering the Latin of it, which was impressive. It seems I'm not the only lover of Latin. Anyways, I took them through a few pieces of poetry that I like, one of them being 'You Start Dying Slowly' by Martha Medeiros. There was this young girl in the group with black fingernails, black clothes, piercings – very Goth-esque. I really like that look as it happens, but it can sometimes be indicative of a dwelling in the dark stage with young people. Goth is a little angsty, a little rebellious, a little edgy, while being withdrawn by its general nature, I find. She had that walk about her which girls with low self-confidence have. The one where they lean their head forward slightly rather than holding it upright, in a bid not to stand out too much, the one that young girls who haven't realised how pretty they are yet often take on. It's a very human, very feminine thing that I've often pondered as unnatural. In nature, flowers never turn their heads away from the sun.

It was my first time working with sixth formers so I wasn't quite sure how I'd gone down there. I remember thinking how close they were to my eldest Son's age, how he is often embarrassed by my eccentricities and can find my ideas quite odd. I wasn't sure if they might do also.

I digress, back to the young Goth girl. I got word yesterday that there had been a change in her, and one of her teachers had enquired as to why this change was. It seems that after the workshop with me, she had gone home, pinned the 'You Start Dying Slowly' poem to her 'happy wall', and over the next few days the blackness of her wardrobe had started to dilute, little by little she started to wear bright colours again. She started to find her own way back to her own rainbow, I guess.

Maybe she'd felt some poetic resonance with this part of the poem that tells us how you start dying slowly, "If you do not change your routine,/If you do not wear different colours/Or you do no not speak to those you do not know". Maybe it stopped a little bit of her from dying slowly. I just thought it was lovely that a piece of poetry written by a lady in Brazil had such a dramatic impact on a teenager living on the Wirral. It was nice to be part of that; such experiences stop me dying slowly, too. I suppose, if anything, they bring little parts of me I'd forgotten back to life.

Poetry is a very powerful thing.

Buddy & the psychologist *28th March 2017*

I can be very wrong sometimes; in fact, it's commonplace that, from time to time, pessimistic realism creeps into my bones. Today I was very glad to be wrong.

Buddy's mother and I were summoned to his school to meet a 'psychologist'. Now, my first thought, based on past experience of this was "Here we go, another institutional monkey trying to put a child into a ticky box". While we were in the reception area waiting to go into the meeting, I started to chat to a guy who was also waiting to see somebody; I really liked him, he had a nice gentle way about him. I'm good at getting the feel of people quite quickly, I think. As things turned out, I found out a few minutes later that he was the psychologist that had assessed Buddy. We sat down with him and Buddy's form teacher, and as the meeting was unfolding I began to warm to him more; I realised that this guy had a genuine intention to help Buddy, and also began to realise that he wasn't just a faceless jobsworth. When a person cares about what they do, and cares about others apart from themselves, you can see it in their face, hear it in their voice; their whole being takes on a sort of meditative motion. He'd run a series of tests, different things to assess a child's ability to learn. Buddy should have been averaging between about 55-60 on the scale, but in most cases he was lucky to hit 15-20. Apart from speaking that is, in that he excelled (maybe a genetic inheritance from somebody, I'll leave that there). Buddy's Mum and I weren't defensive as regards his low test scores; we know he's behind and, in many ways, punching above his intellectual weight in mainstream school. But God, does he keep punching and trying. For all of the problems he has encountered due to his heart condition, I think sometimes that it may be because he was given the heart from a lion cub by mistake. Buddy's Mum went on to explain his condition to the psychologist; a history of two heart attacks, a stroke, and major brain damage etc, and how he has amazed everybody just to be able to walk and talk, never mind attempt to read and write at any mainstream school level.

His teacher, however, was defensive after the results were disclosed to us. She was defensive in such a lovely way too, like she felt that she had to fight his corner. She said he just needs a little help, and what he lacks in classroom ability he may be able to catch up with if he was granted that extra help. Then she mentioned him as a human being not a test paper. She recounted how, during Assembly recently, a little girl in the school with Down's Syndrome was distressed and crying. She told us all how Buddy had become distressed too, and how he wouldn't rest or sit down until he'd gone to check on her and try to make her feel better. She said, "He's just so loving and compassionate, I don't know what I'll do next year when he's not in my class, I just love him." I could see her starting to fill up, and was close to it myself through seeing how much she thought of him. She told how she knew he'd never try to hurt anyone on purpose, and that all he wants to do is make people smile. We could all see what she was saying. She was emphasising how, although he may not be able to draw a line through the circle with the most dots, his worth as a tiny person far outweighs that. He becomes an inspiration through his loving nature, through wanting to make the bad things good, and through striving to heal and protect those within his environment.

By the end of the meeting we all got it, psychologist included. Butterflies flap their wings to different altitudes, soar to differing heights, but that doesn't make the ones that fly low any less colourful or beautiful. It just adds to how unique they are. We all knew that we were dealing with a special little person that needs just a touch more help in certain areas. It transpired that a plan was put into place to apply for funding for extra help, and an application will be made. I'm not sure how that will go, but at least we now know that there are professional people fighting his corner who 'get' him and care about his wellbeing. Again, realism and knowledge of politically instigated cuts tell me that it won't be cut and dry getting what he obviously needs, but at least it's going in the direction we all want.

I was glad to be wrong today, I've never been gladder. I was expecting a grey suit with an agenda and instead met a real live person with a willingness to help children. It makes a difference, instils a little faith and, more importantly, gives hope.

Stan & Mary *27th April 2017*

I love people's stories, and I heard one the other day I just had to put down in writing. I'm a great believer that there are stories everywhere if you have eyes to see and ears to listen. This one came second-hand to me from someone who has those eyes and ears. I do some work in a nursing home and one of the girls who works there watches this story unfold every day...

Stan and Mary have been married for over fifty years and now, in the twilight of their lives, they both have quite severe dementia. So much so, that one does not know who the other is and vice versa. Unable to care for themselves, they have both ended up in separate rooms in the same residential nursing home. Of a morning, Stan wakes around eight o'clock; he becomes restless, paces the floor and is a little aggressive at times. It is as though something is troubling him, but he can't quite figure out what it is. He goes down to breakfast. Mary wakes a little later and comes for breakfast at around ten o'clock every day. When she enters the room, Stan's eyes light up; he goes from anxious to infatuated with this lady he thinks he has never set eyes on before, this lady that Stan thinks only just walked into his life that very morning. He rises to his feet and is drawn to her like a magnet, takes the seat closest to Mary at the table, and just stares at her in awe. His whole body language changes and a serenity envelops him as he takes his place by her side. It's as though he's found the lost piece of the jigsaw of his life that was missing when he climbed out of bed that morning, and he can now be at peace. If you ask Mary "Do you know who this man is?" she can't remember his name, but she goes bashful and coy, and starts to blush; she obviously still thinks that this man is very handsome. Mirroring this, Stan thinks she is the most beautiful lady he has ever laid eyes on. After breakfast, Mary moves to her armchair and Stan follows, like a shadow to Mary's form. They sit together all day, neither knowing who the other is, neither knowing that they have a past together, or a family, or even where they are; they just know that they are in the right place when they are together. They get to fall in love for the first time every morning, but then forget each other as they drift off to sleep each evening. Perhaps they merge lovingly into one another's dreaming. It's like a perpetual cycle of romance and forgetting. Mary took a fall a couple of weeks ago and bruised her arm quite badly; when Stan saw this he kept holding her hand and kissing her arm for hours in an attempt to heal her.

My friend who witnessed this became quite overwhelmed and started crying. Presumed as maybe too sensitive by the other carers, she told me that she just couldn't understand why they couldn't all realise the enormity of what was occurring; how Stan and Mary were obvious proof that love is something that is beyond mind and knowledge. In her words, that "love is something spiritual". I think that's very true. I hypothesise that perhaps love is a frequency that is felt, witnessed and lived, rather than a thought or process. It is spiritual as she said; but maybe also chemical, sensory and intuitively led, certainly guided by a sixth sense that becomes awakened in the presence of a soul mate. Somebody said once that 'love is hard' and I disagreed; relationships yes! But not love. It's the barriers inside us that make 'loving' hard, psychological memory being probably the greatest barrier. Emotional debris in the form of cardiac scars due to past hurts, resentment, bitterness and judgement, all causing resistance to us loving unconditionally. Psychological memory is what Mary and Stan seem to be totally free from, and (just maybe) that makes their love even more beautiful than ours in a strange way.

Because they can love without memory or imagination, love in that very moment, every single day, from breakfast until bed.

Mr Willis *5th May 2017*

Upon starting secondary school, we met a lot of characters. One was Mr Willis. A rumour had circulated throughout the school that Mr Willis had trained to be a Christian monk, but was kicked out of the convent for masturbating. I'm not sure how the rumour started, however the nickname 'Wanker Willis' was adopted and admittedly I was one of those kids who would occasionally (no, that's a lie, more like habitually) shout 'Wanker Willis!' from behind a hedgerow or fence, and then run like hell before he could recognise who it was. Weirdly enough though, Mr Willis never gave chase or got angry. He just kept walking the same path, in the same way, purposefully, head held high like a man with something important to deliver. My (and our) abuse continued for a number of years until we realised it didn't get a reaction, and then we went about the more serious teenage pastimes of accosting bus stop windows, fighting, getting drunk, having underage sex, and writing our names in stolen marker pen on anything that didn't move (or had stopped moving for more than 30 seconds). When we entered sixth form, we were offered different options for A level, and one of them was 'Christian Theology'. Now, I had no interest in this subject whatsoever, although it did have a few draws to it. Firstly, you sat in a circle of comfortable armchairs discussing things rather than writing at a desk. Secondly, there wasn't much homework. Thirdly, nobody minded if you fell asleep! This class was lectured by Mr Willis, and I actually felt a little cheeky applying for the option given my years of insulting the poor guy. I was hard-faced enough to stroll in and take my place on those comfy armchairs though. I was even cheeky enough during one lesson to ask if it was true that he'd been expelled from a convent. As it transpired, it wasn't at all true. He explained how, when he was younger, he had decided to dedicate his life to serving God, but as his training progressed he had realised that he really wanted a wife and children one day, and this wouldn't be possible if he stayed with the church. He gave up his vocational dedication to the Catholic Church, started a family, and became a RE teacher instead.

That day, 'Wanker Willis' became 'Mr Willis', and sometime after that he let me call him 'John'. Something else changed also; John's class became the highlight of my study days. John introduced me to Kant, Descartes, Nietzsche and Aristotle. I fell in love with philosophy and theology, I learnt about utilitarianism and discussed it's social, moral and rational implications. I learnt about the cognitive acrobatics that could unfold within my mind while discussing such topics. John taught us how to meditate, spoke about the power of prayer, told us stories of saints, mystics and martyrs. He taught us of Greek mythology and Demigods. We questioned a God of form, along with Devils, Angels and Demons. For the first time in our school career, a teacher treated us as adults, and not just schoolchildren. John opened doors for our minds to step through and explore, as aimlessly or as purposefully as we cared to venture. John also opened up his heart and mind to us like a library, a lifetime of spiritual seeking and study, of philosophy and atheist treatises designed to test a person's faith, were opened up at our disposal.

The arrogance of my youth and my own aversion to Catholicism led to contention between John and I on many topics relating to belief, but it was always a discussion, never an argument. I always admired his faith, perhaps envied it in a peculiar way. He knew his path and I was still lost in the flux of it all (in many ways I still am, I suppose), but the spiritual journey is lifelong and beyond, I guess.

John believed I was intelligent, a compliment I didn't ever feel comfortable receiving. He made comment about how I hid it by acting like a clown. He was very right of course, it was easier to have my academic potential lay dormant beneath a braggadocio facade than realise it. I was torn between two worlds at the time; a schoolboy and a doorman. Enrolled onto nightclub doors at the age of sixteen (much too young), I was studying theology in the afternoon and witnessing the underbelly of Liverpool's violent and nefarious club scene of an evening. I remember on one occasion (I must have been about seventeen), explaining the ontological argument to two heavily steroidal doormen with a distinct absence of neck, while standing on the door of a nightclub. An agitated young lady then approached us to explain how "The fella over there just grabbed me fanny!", then all of a sudden we seemed to be punching fuck out of a group of lads, that were so high on cocaine that we struggled to knock them out, and I had to opt for sleeper holds to convey them into the obligatory state of unconsciousness that we were expected to impose as punishment for a rogue 'minge grab' in those days. I didn't ever get to finish the main points of the ontological argument. I became a closet philosopher, took on the nickname 'The Boston Strangler', and kept the more intellectual side of me tucked away. Lad culture is like that; in the company of other alpha males it's easier to be a thug than a philosopher. 'If you can't fuck it or fight it then discard it' is the general rule of thumb. So many males mask all sensitivity, artistry and intelligence in a bid not to look in any way vulnerable to the pack.

John saw something in me I wasn't ready to acknowledge in myself as yet. He believed in me, and that's one of the greatest gifts a human being can bestow onto another. I just wasn't ready to accept that gift in those years.

A few years ago, I went to see John; I believed he had spiritual knowledge and I was seeking answers, brushes with clairvoyance and numerous other spiritual experiences were going on in my life that I couldn't make sense of, and this caused me to seek his counsel. John helped me, John had become a friend. The guy I used to call a wanker from behind hedgerows had by then, not only earned my trust, but also my complete admiration; enough for me to confide in him that I was questioning my sanity. John was a great man, if anything I was the wanker on the other side of the hedgerow. But that's what young boys do; they wank a lot and shout insults. I'm sort of growing out of it a little as I move further towards my forties, but admittedly both of those pastimes still shadow me a little.

Over the past couple of days, I've learnt of two people I know passing. They say that death comes in threes, and this afternoon I had a returned email from John. I sent an email to him a few weeks ago in a bid to catch up, his daughter wrote the response. John lost a battle to cancer in February and I didn't know. I loved John. Great teachers are one in a million.

I was talking to the angels last night, asking for a little help for someone who's lost somebody, and it's a little comforting for me to know John was listening with them. I was thinking just now that he'd be proud of me. I've sort of found my heart's path, working with children. New avenues have opened up to work in schools and with children in social services care and disabled children. Maybe he's helping me along, perhaps I can be somebody else's John one day. Inspire a child, lift them, believe in them, and give them that gift he gave to me, whether they are ready to receive it or not. It's always there when they are ready to accept it. I'm going to accept his compliment to me now I think, as his leaving present to me. And even if these kids I'm working with think I'm a wanker at first, I'll just keep walking the same path in the same way, purposefully, with my head held high like a man with something important to deliver. Like John showed me how to do, because I know one good teacher can change a life.

Night & God bless John.
Love G X

Flame & biscuit

16th May 2017

When was a kid, I remember always being hungry of a night. My Nan would call me 'Gutsy McGinty' and tell me "Your eyes are bigger than your belly". I used to sit there putting my two palms to the width of my stomach and then to the width of an eye, just to check if she was right. Then performing the same exercise to an amused grandparental audience to prove how wrong they were. Nans can say funny things when you're little. They had this big, beige biscuit tin in the kitchen cupboard. It, at one time, resided in the bottom cupboard, but following a number of quite ruthless and brutal Viking-style biscuit tin raids by oneself as a toddler, it was graduated to the safety of the top cupboard. I still remember scaling onto the kitchen worktop as quietly as I could to break into it while they were watching TV in the living room. I'd be there on my knees, in the dark, surreptitiously lowering it onto the work surface with all the gentle grace of a midwife. The silence seemed thunderously loud. When a child is up to no good their adrenaline kicks in and creates a heightened sensory awareness. I could hear my own heart beat in my ears, lower my breathing rate to that of a hibernating amphibian, and smell an adult alighting an armchair from quarter of a mile away. The pure white dishcloths embalming themselves in bleach ready for work the next day would float there like water angels, playing silent witness to my childhood sins.

Once I was there kneeling on the worktop, there was the vacuum seal to break; those old biscuit tins were as airtight as a sarcophagus, and breaking that seal would be the equivalent of a bomb going off to my heightened senses, causing spikes of adrenaline to run to my knees, arms and fingertips. I'd push up a little on the flanged edge using my two thumbs, while cupping it with both palms and knees to avoid it sliding about. All of my ingenuity was applied to avoid an acoustic discrepancy that may tell-tale on me. A little push upwards on one side of the tin, then a little on the opposite, then on the quarters of its circumference, until... 'POUP!' I got to reach in and seize my treasure. He who dares wins when it comes to biscuit tin raiding. I'd had to evolve as I grew in years; move from Viking pillaging to sophisticated cat burglary. Such is childhood crime, and all crime in general really, it alters to suit the conditions of the time.

Anyways, after I put Buddy in bed tonight I closed my eyes for a minute to rest and drifted off into a dreamy nap, I'm not sure where I went, I think I may have gone to my Nan's. 20 Sanderling Road, Kirkby was my happy place as a child. Don't get me wrong, there was no need for the NSPCC at my Mum's, it was just that Mary & Joe's was where my heart lived. When I woke up from my snooze, Buddy was still rattling about his room, not sleeping. Generally, once he's in bed he's not allowed out until he falls asleep, but then I thought "Maybe he's hungry". So, I went in, and just as he was expecting me to tell him that he better get to sleep because he has school in the morning, I asked him if he wanted some toast. Bewilderedly he said yes, so I carried him downstairs and he sat on the kitchen worktop as I prepared it. But he looked a bit cold there in just his pyjamas, so I moved him to the sofa, issued a fluffy blanket, and put the fire on. As we sat there together, he told me about the men and women he could see dancing in the fire; unfortunately, my eyes are a little too adult to see them properly now, so he had to tell me about them and how beautifully they danced. I used to see those people dance in my Nan's fire, I know I did, I had the same magic eyes back then. I wish us grown-ups could buy spectacles to give us that vision back. Imagine a skip full of televisions at the end of every street, and people actually talking to each other, telling stories and watching fires. He asked where the people who danced in the fire went as they disappeared up the chimney. Between Buddy and I we figured out the secret of that, so I thought I'd share it here. You see, fire is born on Earth and once a human tells a story to the flames the spirits in the fire are allowed to travel up to Heaven and burn with the stars. They tell the stars our stories; stars love Earth stories, and that makes them happy so they shine brighter. I think we solved one of the mysteries of the universe there. We also worked out why fires and storytelling are so important to humans.

Lest we forget.

Sweet shop Saṃsāra *11th June 2017*

Sometimes on the way home from work, I stop and buy myself some jellies. At thirty-eight, you'd think I might have grown out of that, but no. It's like a ritualistic thing from childhood. I love the whole experience; the survey, perusal and acquisition of them. The thirty second exchange of pleasantries over a slab of newspapers with the Hindu lady, who probably thinks I'm buying them for my kids. Holding the door open for the little old lady, who turns up magically on cue, every time, just as you go to step outside.

"Thanks Son."

"Welcome Girl."

Then, I open them as I'm walking along, stuffing a couple into my mouth as I head for the van. Today I was a bit divided over the pink mushrooms or the sugar dummies, so I probably walked ten steps in dilemma before deciding to eat half a bag of mushrooms on the way to the van, then pop the sugar dummies before I started the engine. I'm on those three-for-a-pound mix-bags at the minute, I can always pick two really easily, but struggle to decide on the third. You probably know how that is, or maybe not.

Anyways, today was a bit shit in places, but I bought some sweets and it cheered me up a little.

A year of tears & a taxi *13th June 2017*

I was thinking today about this guy I met around ten years ago, a taxi driver. I was travelling South East Asia. Now, it's very rare that I'll take an air-conditioned taxi while travelling those parts, however I was running late to cross the Border into Cambodia and was feeling rather too delicate to be playing rugged explorer. If memory serves me correctly, the night before I'd gotten into a vodka drinking session with a German banker, a Dutch guy who was ex-Special Forces, and a Ladyboy who was comically regaling tales of her bad luck through falling in love with handsome Farangs without any money. At one point, the coquettish Dutch guy had turned his pockets out in a display of poverty to console her, and I'd shouted to him to "Turn it into an elephant!" which he did, and in doing so earned himself a drunken round of applause and a free shot. Maybe the Special Forces Farang and the broken-hearted Katou fell in love that night, got married and lived happily ever after. What a story that would make. One thing is for sure though, he'll never beat her at pool. She was mustard, she rinsed the three of us that night, and got all her drinks bought for her trouble.

The next morning, I had the most atrocious hangover, not helped by an unusually tumultuous ferry crossing from Ko-Chang to the mainland. At some point I'd opted for a taxi, mostly for comfort while suffering a bout of hangover anxiety and dread, but also to make up some lost travelling time. I wasn't particularly receptive to chat, but the driver spoke really good English, seemed like a nice guy, and at some point had managed to coax a conversation from the bereft ghost that was once oneself, now almost anaemically haunting the passenger seat beside of him. I asked him if he had any children and then found I had inadvertently (and quite innocently) stumbled upon an emotional landmine. He told me his story. He told me how he had only ever loved one woman; from the moment he met her as a child he knew that he wanted to be with her always. His eyes sparkled when he tried to put into words how beautiful he thought she was. He told me that she had a beautiful face and a beautiful soul, and how he would never love another woman as long as he lived. About five years before I had queasily stepped into his taxi, they were expecting their first child, a little boy. There were some complications during the labour, and he sadly recounted how both his love and his Son had crossed over into the next life due to birthing complications, and that he was now all alone in this life. Then he said something to me, and I'll always remember this; he said, "I cried," then he turned to me, held eye contact, held one finger up in front of his face and said, "For one whole year I cried, one whole year." He looked back to the road as he drove and continued speaking. "In the morning I would wake and I would cry all day until I fell asleep. The next morning I would cry again until the night; I didn't work, I didn't eat hardly a thing, I just cried for one whole year. And at the end of that year, I stopped and started my life again; I had used up all of my tears." Now, you may be reading this thinking that the man may have been a little out, that it's very unlikely for a person to cry for exactly one year, and I wouldn't blame you for doubting. All I can say is this; that at that time, in that taxi, I believed him. The man had truth in his voice and he was speaking from a place that honoured his own heart. To this day I still believe every word he said, however incredible that may sound. I do believe that he cried for exactly one year and then stopped.

I thought back to my Nan's funeral, as that was the last time I could remember crying in public. I must have been about ten or eleven I think (don't quote me on that, as I have very little concept of time). As I stepped out of the funeral car, it all got a bit real for me. I'd seen the coffin and nearly broken down in the kitchen at her house, looked at my Granddad who swiftly adjusted his black tie then half-filled a half-pint glass with whisky and downed it in one go for breakfast. He didn't cry. (As a child, I didn't notice any of the men cry that day). When we arrived at the church, I stepped out of the funeral car and I cried, I cried like I had never cried before, I broke my heart sobbing right there in the open grey no-man's land of the Sacred Heart Church car park. I kept thinking how it couldn't be real. How could a childhood eternity of hugs, Ovaltine and love come to an end in a grey church car park? How could she leave us all alone? I looked to the black-suited males around me for answers; they seemed like giants with glum faces, but, no tears? Peter Lamb, a distant relative, broke form from the statuesque mourners watching the coffin being lifted out of the hearse to begin its journey onwards towards the alter. He came over to comfort me with a hug and held me until I was ready to walk in. I'll always love Peter for that, I'll never forget how much that meant. As I sat there in the church taking in the pungent fumes of that bastard Catholic incense (a smell I still hate even to this very day), one of the things that occurred to me was this; I wasn't a man yet, because I'd cried.

That's something that carried through into later life to some degree, and to use a Johnny Cash line, "My fists got hard and my wits got keen". Certainly, as a younger man I was far more likely to punch somebody in the face than cry, it was much easier, I found. I have this theory that maybe the much repeated 'Big boys don't cry' line was an ingenious yet erroneous marketing ploy, made up by a firm that held the monopoly on manufacturing internal doors. I couldn't even begin to contemplate how many six-panel living room doors have buckled beneath a straight right from a frustrated male who just couldn't put words to his frustration, or find it within himself to drop a tear. Brilliant for door sales, but terrible for the families living in those homes; especially as it's not only doors that those frustrations have historically been vented upon, but in many cases helpless women and children. Unfortunately, it still goes on, behind closed doors with knuckle marks in. It's a very fear-based society for males, and a certain straitjacketed, unrealistic ideal of how men should behave as regards which emotions we can and can't display, while still retaining a perceived masculine persona, has certainly been the cause of much unnecessary suffering.

The reason I was thinking about that taxi driver today was that I wanted to broach something with Buddy. You see, Buddy and I were at dinner with some friends last week and a new boyfriend of an old friend said "Big boys don't cry" to Buddy. Before I could interject, another female friend had quickly silenced him by saying how ridiculous that was. She explained how her Son had suffered with extreme anxiety until he was twenty-seven, and the biggest cause of it was feeling that he wasn't allowed to cry because he was a man. To give the guy who said "Big boys don't cry" a little credit, he then backed off on the statement and said "It was just something my Uncles always told me while growing up", and explained how he had never thought about it much in that way. This left my female friend feeling like she'd exorcised that demon statement from the dinner table comfortably. My own response would have just been to say "Sometimes I cry", but with the guy now back in his box and repentant, I felt I'd forgone the opportunity, and also felt his statement had already come up against enough impassioned and fiery opposition to cancel it out. So, I left it there in a gracious bid to let the topic reach rigor mortis without any further fireworks.

Anyway, I sat down with Buddy tonight and we talked about how it's OK to cry, and how even Daddy cries sometimes. Just to reinforce that he gets that. I believe that the human body has its own innate wisdom in the way that it functions, and if it wants to move or act in a certain way, then it is unhealthy to suppress that. I also genuinely believe that if we can (in some way) move past this generational reinforcement of the doctrine that boys aren't supposed to cry, then the males of ensuing generations to follow could potentially endure better standards of mental health and be less violent towards others, maybe we could even stop some suicides. I'm no psychologist; I could be miles out on this, maybe the old ways are best for other reasons that I don't quite get. But all I can do is be honest with my own children based on my own experience. In our house, crying is OK for boys, and nobody in our house will ever think any less of you for dropping a tear in joy, anger or sorrow. If nothing else it'll save money on doors, and maybe also stop them taking up weird habits like writing poetry.

But that's OK too, if they really, really have to.

Dickhead blocker *18th June 2017*

I was really happy with Buddy tonight because he came home with a pink Trolls magazine. That may sound weird, but there's a good reason behind it. Buddy loves going for a magazine; he can't even read the bloody things and they are extortionately priced, but I think buying one makes him feel like a grown-up. Anyways, sometimes on a Tuesday, my brother takes him for a mag. When they got back this time, my brother sort of apologetically says, "I did try to talk him out of buying the pink one, but he wouldn't have it." I just smiled and said, "That's brilliant." I told him the story about when Buddy and I were in Blackpool and he picked a pink toy. The lady in shop said quite loudly (and with some gusto), "You don't want that one, it's pink! Pink is a g—" and at that point, before she could say that pink was a girl's colour, I stopped her dead. I said quite curtly in a low tone, "Look love, he wants the pink one, and I want him to have the pink one if he wants the pink one, now the only person here who seems to not want him to have the pink one is you. Can he just have the fucking pink one please?"

Maybe I was a bit short with her, but I was tired and it seemed like a lot of bullshit over a toy. The woman just passed him the pink toy, Buddy and I both said thank you to her, and off we popped all happy with the pink one. Dead easy isn't it? My brother got it then; just makes him happy, nothing else matters. Nobody means any harm by it, it's just social gender conditioning that gets passed down and people aren't conscious of. In French, I believe it's the other way around; pink is the masculine colour and blue is the feminine colour. Colour is in no way indicative of gender or sexuality, that's just a stupid belief that's been perpetuated culturally through ignorance. I was proud tonight because Buddy didn't sway and he stuck to his guns. I can just imagine my brother now, standing in the Tesco saying things like "You don't really want the pink one, do you? Look at this amazing blue one with cars all over it!" and Bud's being like "Fuck you Uncs, I like pink, I'm having it!" In Buddy language of course, which has less swearing. I hope.

I encountered the same sort of thing not long ago. Buddy loves his Liverpool kit. He's got no idea how good a team Liverpool Football Club are or where they are in the league table. He's also got no prejudices about any other football teams, or any other children wearing other team's kits. We were in the park and a grown man walks over to us, points his finger at Buddy, and (probably quite harmlessly in his own mind) exclaims, "You've got the wrong colour kit on there lad, it should be blue!" Then Buddy looks at the guy puzzled, then looks to me a little self-consciously as if to ask "What's this guy talking about Dad?" So, I say to the guy (just out of Buddy's earshot), "Don't be a twat, he's six." My eyes probably flashing like the sharp steel of a sword, the guy walks off, probably a little intimidated by me. Sorry, but fuck him. The man means no harm, I know, but I just want to nip it in the bud as curtly and quickly as possible, and have my little boy go back to being happy, not confused or self-conscious in any way. Because this is what I see; I see it from Buddy's perspective. Imagine you're six years old, three foot tall, and innocent to the world. Then a so called 'grown-up' you don't know walks up to you while you're sporting your favourite football kit quite happily. The grown-up is six foot tall, approximately 15 stone, and forty years old. The grown-up points his finger down at you, the child, and says the words "wrong kit". I just haven't got time to explain to that grown-up how 'twatty' that is from a child's perspective; how potentially intimidating that could be if I wasn't standing there beside him, or how it could potentially take the shine off a little boy's joy in wearing his favourite colour kit. Now, I probably am being a little overprotective – a little curt, yes – but I'm working on a different level that I haven't got time to explain to people who aren't on that level. Where I'm working from is this; to me, adults aren't really that important when compared to children. You get one childhood. It should be filled with joy and wonder and innocence for as long as practicably possible, without that experience being hindered by dickheads. That's my job as a Dad; I'm a dickhead blocker. It's just business that I attend to without the need to explain it to anyone, educate anyone, or enlighten them on the way I view the world. If I love you, I'll explain, but I can't educate everyone, I haven't got time.

The other level I work on is this: a belief that if anybody is pursuing their own happiness and not hurting anybody else, be that child or adult, just leave them the fuck alone. The guy with purple trousers, the guy with weird hair, the guy who wears a dress, the woman who wants to be a guy, the ten year old boy who wants to wear high heels, the ten year old girl who wants to play with an Action Man not a Barbie; just leave them the fuck alone. Give them heels and Action Men and purple trousers and mad haircuts because you can only like what you like, and you can only be what you are. If they move away from this they will become desperately unhappy. Buddy was happy with his pink magazine. Me and my brother now are happy for him too.

I'm very proud that he stood his ground tonight in Tesco.

Sir cares *19th June 2017*

Lovely things happen sometimes. I was doing a poetry session in a senior school, and I asked all of the kids to write a piece. Their teacher, who's with me asks, "Sir, can I write a poem?" Obviously, I said I'd love him to. Anyway, I watch him take a breath, pause and thoughtfully start to write. I thought "This guy needs this, this is what I'm here for, to facilitate this," but I wasn't expecting it from the teacher. Then, come read around time, he delivers this amazing piece of poetry about what loss meant to him. The kids are blown away, and start applauding him without even being prompted. I thought, "Wow, the kids aren't just happy with the poetry, they are genuinely proud of him." He went on to explain what the poem was about; his sister had terminal cancer, and his mother was caring for her. His mother died of a heart attack while looking after his sister, and within a short space of time he lost them both. I think the kids were proud of him because he had the courage to show himself, show a little of his story, his humanity. Just for a second, we all fell in love a little bit with this beautiful sensitive guy with a very sad story. We all got to see him in a different light. 'Sir' became a person with a heart, and not just a suit with a lesson plan. In short, Sir was 'Real' for a moment. I spoke to him afterwards, and he said that he was nervous about reading it out, but saw what I was trying to do and how open I was being with the kids about my own story, including experiences of poor mental health, and how writing helped. He said they need to see that we're all human. I believe that he's right.

Anyway, that's something that happened.

Bad Buddy lives *20th June 2017*

Bad Buddy made an appearance today and we had some kick-offs and tantrums. So, just before bed, when it was all calm, I hatched my masterplan to try to eradicate these phenomena. Because I'm really clever like that...

"Buddy."

"Ye."

"We need to talk."

"Why?"

"We need to talk about Bad Buddy."

Buddy goes quiet, and I start my cunning plan...

"Bad Buddy has been showing up a lot lately."

"Ye."

"I think it's time we got shut of him."

"Will you get shut of me?"

"No, I think just Bad Buddy needs to go."

"Don't you like him?"

"Not really, no."

"But do you love him?"

"Ye, I love him, but he's very naughty."

"But he's still a Buddy, isn't he?"

I go quiet and ponder how this one got away from me, and how my cunning plan now sits in cinders at the foot of the bed.

Buddy then looks at me and asks, "You can't get shut of a Buddy if you love him, can you?"

"No, you're right, we can't."

"So, can we keep Bad Buddy?"

"Yes Son."

I take back what I said about being clever, I was just psychologically flanked by a six year old.

Great day today. I took a couple of performance poets into one of my school groups, the kids loved them and asked loads of questions. I really felt like the poets inspired them to express, and not only that but to express themselves positively. Even if what you are writing about is sad, expression is always positive I think, it helps you make sense of the world around you. This week was week seven of an eight week course, and today a kid in the class posed the question "What is the sound of smoke?" I was really proud of the young lad for asking this type of question for a number of reasons. Lyndsay Price, one of the poets, told him that to her it was "the sound of a whisper". I said it could be "the sound of a shadow falling", and the teacher said that to him it was "the hiss of a snake".

Today was part of a pilot I've been running to get children writing and performing their own poetry. I fell pretty lucky; I fell upon a school that was open-minded as regards art to pitch the idea to, I spoke passionately enough about why I wanted to do it, and they gave me a chance. They dedicated an hour a week of lesson time over eight weeks. Now, it's not often schools will pull kids out of maths/science and other less 'arty' subjects to write poetry, so I took it as a big deal. Not only that, but I was also an unknown to them at the start, and they were taking a big chance on me based on seeing that I was passionate about helping kids express themselves to aid their wellbeing, states of mental health and emotional growth. I keep looking for ways to inspire and encourage them to write from their chests, not their heads, and it's hard; the whole education system is stacked against what I'm doing. It's factual rather than poetic, intellectual rather than intuitive, and information-based rather than artistic.

Sometimes leading the sessions can be like bashing my head against a brick wall, and during others it's pure alchemy. The first week I asked them "What colour is love?", then asked them "How much does a teardrop weigh?" There was a bit of talking between themselves and a lot of blank faces. I told them that their friends won't have the answer to give them, that it can't be found in a book or googled, that every child in the room may have a different answer, and that none of the answers could be wrong, but they would have to shut their eyes to find their own right answer. I doubt they've ever been asked to do this in school before and I know how hard it is to try if it's unfamiliar, but some of them did and now, later on in the course, most of them are. That's why I was proud today when that young boy posed a 'poetic' question. He was starting to get it; that smoke can have a sound if you are a writer, it can have a feel or a gender, even an identity in personification. Poetic license was dawning upon him.

I was thinking the other week that I can only take them to the airlock though, and it's up to them whether or not they wish to travel into their own inner-space. So, last week, I called the class the 'Astronaut session'. I explained to the kids that the word 'Astronaut' is made up of two Greek words, 'Astron' meaning 'Star', and 'Naut' meaning 'Sailor' or 'to sail'. I told them that in the same way that an astronaut travels the outer universe, as writers we are offered the opportunity to navigate and explore our own inner universes. I asked them to become star-sailors in their own right.

And that may sound crazy, but I believe that it's actually starting to work.

Mrs S *7th July 2017*

There's this nursing home I do electrical work in, I love being around the old people there. I've always had an affinity with old people and children, maybe because they are so alike in many ways. Adults are my least favourite group of people, I think. I do get a bit distracted at times and have to get my arse back to doing the electrical work. I was on the dementia ward the other day, I was helping some old dear with a jigsaw while also in the middle of changing a fuse board, and then realised I better get the power back on quick and stop jigsawing before someone spots me and complains. The dementia ward is probably my favourite place, they all make perfect sense to me, it's like an oasis of sanity in a mad world. My favourite is this lady called… well, I won't say her name, I'll call her Mrs S. She's ninety now, but she's still got fire in her belly. When Callum (my apprentice) and I walk past, she points at us and says to the girls looking after her, "Look! Men! Men! Get an eye-full!" She's the only one you'll find having a sneaky cigarette with the staff in the smoking hut, a proper rebel, always casing the place to try and escape. She did escape the other day, I was really proud of her when I heard the news of that. She didn't get far, but I was really glad she had because I'd watched her plan it for ages. I felt extremely guilty another day, because I saw her slipping out and had to say something to the staff. She'd figured out how to open the fire exit at the side and ghosted it shiftily until the coast was clear, then darted. I'm not generally a snitch, so I found it really hard to inform on her, however I was scared she might hurt herself or get lost. You see, some days are different. Some days, she's a little bit more confused, and when we stop for our talks she holds my arm that little bit tighter, like someone that's a little scared and wants to feel safe. On other days, she's more than a bit confused and gets teary; she wants to go home, but doesn't quite know where home is. She covers it well though, she's clever enough to distract from questions rather than answer them if she doesn't know the answer. She thinks I haven't spotted it, but I have; she's very proud. When she's down, it makes me a little down, too. I like her when she's being ballsy. I sort of have these lovely visions in my head of her one day throwing a water fountain through the window and escaping across the fields, and them finding her a week or so later, card-sharking with a joint in her mouth, during a late night lock-in at a local pub. One where everybody knows her name, even if she can't remember theirs.

I was just thinking about her, I admire her a lot.

Trainspotting 2 *10th July 2017*

I was watching *Trainspotting 2* tonight, and couldn't help but feel a little nostalgic. What a film the original was, it was iconic. A wide-eyed look into the filthy underbelly of Edinburgh's scag culture with sex, violence, death and drugs, sliding between the rooms and stairways of high-rise buildings. Broken hearts and dirty needles littering the backdrop of misguided youthful hedonism, not glamorised as much as held up to the light of scrutiny with all the genitals to be examined. Watching the sequel, I felt a sort of closeness with the characters, not that I've ever lived that addict life, but rather because they were a huge part of my growing up, my teen years. I felt like I knew the characters and genuinely wanted to see how they had progressed over the past two decades as people. In a way, actually cared about them. Such is teen sentiment, I guess. *T2* is sympathetic to that I think, it explains where they have been and who they have become. Some changed a lot, some changed a little, but they all retained that diamond-hard council estate grit deep inside of them, and I loved that. Not as pungent or as shocking as the first film, but it didn't have to be, it shocked us so well twenty years ago that it had well made its point and therefore could move a lot more smoothly as the storyline unfolded. What was also nice was the way in which the new storyline touched on some of the darker matter from the original *Trainspotting*, from a place of retrospect. With the characters looking back having had two decades to reflect on where they had gone wrong and why, guilt and regret still there in many cases, and that's a big part of life not often covered too well in film making. The sequel gave the makers a chance to run over this with a great deal of finesse. It was a really warm film for me to watch, touching even.

I was never a big reader back then, but picked up a lot of Irvine Welsh's books after watching *Trainspotting*. He's one sick puppy him, twisted and conjoined, but an amazing descriptive writer who takes you to dark places you could never have visited without his imagination opening its gates for you. The novels *Acid House, Filth* and *Ecstasy* probably being my three favourites. If you want kids to stay away from drugs, just read them those. Highs written about yes, but the lows, so low you find you may have underestimated the depths of human depravity. Welsh deals in excess, in the exponentially expanding darkness that can consume the human mind and spirit as an addict or user. He shows us how far from God an angel can fall with a needle in his arm. Not only that, he explores sexual perversions and lusts like an artist paints on canvas, which I really like if I'm honest, but then, sort of don't like, also. His work is very often 'sugar and shite' to the reader's/viewer's pallet. I was quite glad he took his foot off the gas a little for *T2* and was easy on us this time. I thought it was a great sequel.

Anyways, was just thinking about it and writing helps me do that.

Sentimental psychometry *12th July 2017*

I'm terribly sentimental I guess, I have this thing about objects and small gifts. Could be anything; a stone I found at the top of a waterfall on a day my friend took me out is one example. I collect stones, I have them from all over the country, all over the world. I collect them from places I travel to and ask other people to bring me a stone back as a gift if they are going anywhere. Stones aren't expensive, obviously, but I just tell the person to "Find me the right stone, the perfect stone, you'll know it when you see it". Weirdly enough, they always do. I have little pieces of the world scattered all over my home, but that's not what it's about. It is about the thought that went into bringing that stone back to me. The simple fact that somebody stood in another place and time holding a thought for me, I find that comforting.

The house is sprinkled with trinkets and unusual paraphernalia; a bookmark, or a crystal from a past lover, the picture of the tiger who came to tea that my friend Helen surprised me with one day (we were at an art fair one Christmas, she bought it while I wasn't looking and hid it in her bag), a book from somebody who isn't with us anymore, or a letter received to say thanks for being there for me while I was ill. Sometimes, I'll just touch one of those things and remember that person and smile. Most of the things are, on a monetary level, worthless or worth very little, but to me they're priceless. I have a very poor memory for places been and things done, the when's and where's of life, but I remember people by feeling. Sort of a 'sentimental psychometry', you might say.

Little things eh!

Fucked-up world *15th July 2017*

Buddy can't work out why he has to get up, and says that we should be able to just stay in bed and cuggle. If I'm honest I haven't got a reasonable answer to give him as to why we can't. People need cuggles more than they need to go to school or work; that's just common sense. I've bribed him out of bed with sausages and ketchup now, but it's a fucked-up world.

Even a six year old knows that.

Aeroplanes & ripped kimonos *18th July 2017*

Life's a little funny sometimes, well, people are, I mean. People are very queer things sometimes. In fact, I've always felt a bit sorry for psychiatrists and such-like in attempting to figure out such strange creatures. I should imagine it to be the equivalent of charting the unfathomable depths of a great sea with some Poundland goggles and a pair of armbands on; you're in deep enough to taste the salt and feel the waves, but it's always a guessing game as to what lies beneath. May be dolphins, may be sharks. Some people will put you on a pedestal, and some people will kick its legs out from under you before the treads of your trainers have bit into its surface. I've never quite got that whole 'wanting to bring people down' thing. Don't get me wrong, a good piss-taking from your friends inspires both a good sense of humour and humility in an individual. I'm a big fan of lad culture and piss-taking. In fact, I think that people from Liverpool are number one in the world with a quick-witted one-liner. Sometimes it's a lot darker than that though, and I've witnessed a lot of that, to the point where it has boggled my brains. I love seeing anyone doing well, admire people who try and fall flat on their faces, and admire them even more when they dust themselves off and try again. There're a great many people who enjoy seeing others fall down and I, at least, think they miss the whole point. I find that adversity does something for the human spirit. Like artists, people take pain and use it to turn themselves into an expression, something beautiful. The term 'poetry in motion' could be applied to an old lady escaping from a nursing home, a young boy punching a bully in the face, a grown man stoically smiling through a depression. Art is all around us, in every person we meet; all subjective, maybe not to our taste, but still art, whether we appreciate it as that or not.

I'm also a big fan of people, I believe that most people are genuinely good but, at times, sadly, I'm at a loss with certain folk. I see things in images, in metaphor when I think about them. Maybe there's some fancy name for that, but it's sort of like a 'clairvoyance of concept' that helps me see things for what they are. I see better through mental images and stories for whatever reason (maybe just because I'm weird). In fact, that's certainly the case. I'm as weird as an ironing board on a nudist beach, but I really enjoy that. I love other weird people. I was at a bonfire in the middle of the Welsh woods the other evening, attending the birthday party of a hippie friend, and met this weird guy in a blouse and a ripped kimono-type skirt. I thought, "He looks weird, I'll find out what he's about." Somewhere in between him reciting poetry about a ball of string and dropping ecstasy tablets, he started telling me that he created sculptures; one was of a WW1 fighter plane crashing into a graveyard, with the ghost of the fighter pilot bursting out of the ground. He explained how the nose-dived fighter plane makes the shape of a cross in the graveyard, and we talked ages about it. Weird as fuck he was, I really liked him. Think he was a bit scared of me at first, but then he sort of got I was alright; even offered me some E which I declined, but thought it was very nice of him to offer, as I should imagine amphetamines are in short supply in the middle of a Welsh forest. I'm glad I never got into the whole drugs thing, the Merlot thing serves me well enough. I'm going off-subject here, anyways. I've had dealings with someone lately that seems to not want me to move forward, do well, or be happy. I can't get my head around why, so I started seeing a picture in my mind of two people in jail, and one trying to escape. First prisoner has a plan, but the second prisoner won't help and tries to talk him out of it; even makes a lot of noise to thwart his efforts. When that doesn't work, he snitches to the guards to foil the escape attempt. Resentment then develops between the two captives. Then I sort of figured it out; that the second prisoner is scared of being left behind. The old saying 'misery loves company' is very true. I see it all the time in shit relationships of all kinds, be them friend, family or spouse-like. People all over the place trying to fly on one wing; one wing is love, the other is freedom, but we need both to soar. With only one wing to try and fly with, there's only the saddest type of poetry in motion.

Ye, people are queer things, and sometimes we have to take flight from them before we nose dive into a graveyard, I guess.

The bride who did not smile *30th July 2017*

My friend works in a salon, and she told me a story today about a bride who did not smile. It was her wedding day and she was having her hair and make up done. Everybody in the salon said the woman was strange, and how weird it was, as they'd never know a bride not to smile. When her hair was finished and the stylist asked her how she felt, she merely replied "Thank you for doing my hair". When my friend told me about it, I knew what was wrong with her, she was just sad. Maybe she was sad about something, or sad about many different things, or perhaps she was just sad. To me there isn't anything weird or strange about being sad on any day, even if there is no apparent reason. The conditions on the outside and the conditions on the inside are different, you see, anybody who has been sad enough will know this. I thought about how sadness or depression doesn't recognise Christmases or weddings or holidays or weekends.

Anyways, I wrote a story about it for my friend to help her understand. Sometimes it's easier to explain with a story, and sometimes I think I understand more about sadness than what I'd like to.

Short Story: The bride who did not smile

Nisudra stared into the mirror; red lips, flawless make up, beautiful hair. She viewed the woman in front of her without recognition or judgement. To some degree it was like staring at a picture of somebody else, or perhaps a vision of a past life that she was gently remembering during a death-bed déjà vu. She was cause for some speculation, as this was the first time anybody had known a bride at the salon who did not smile. All of the women said how strange she was, to not smile on her happiest day, the day she marries the man she loves. "Why do you not smile?" the women asked, as they worked to make her even more beautiful. But the only word Nisudra said was "Thank you". She said thank you to each woman as they had finished working on her, and nothing else. And then she stood up and left for her wedding.

Once Nisudra had left, all of the girls started talking about how weird it was, and how strange a bride that did not smile is. Except for one of them; the girl called Nidra who never spoke out. She kept very quiet, but as the other girls went on and on about 'Strange Nisudra', a feeling started to grow inside of her. She was unsure of what it was at first, but it started off as a great sadness and then moved into an overwhelming anger; a protective anger. It was as is if the spirit of a lioness had been awakened inside of her sleeping soul, and she felt the dire need to protest at their insults towards the beautiful bride. How dare they insult a bride on her wedding! How dare they call her strange and weird and mock her! Could they not at all see why the bride did not smile? Did their souls have no eyes and hearts no compassion? Nidra, as if awakened from a sleep, started to talk, her voice – although not loud – rattled like the roar of a lioness carrying fire in her heart, sending out words as shards of energy to cut into the clutter of the other girls' voices and leave them stone-dead muted.

"Would you put up your sun umbrellas to trick the snow into not falling?!" asked Nidra.

The other girls looked shocked and also scared. Where had this voice come from, and what was she saying? Had tiny Nidra gone insane? Nidra continued to speak.

"Because if you think that you can trick the snow with a sun umbrella, then you can easily also trick yourself into believing that every girl will be happy on her wedding day!"

You see, Nidra knew that the conditions on the outside of a person are different from the conditions on the inside of a person, and went on to explain that the bride was just sad, not strange or weird at all, it was just one of her days to be sad. Nisudra's sadness could not be changed by a wedding, any more than a sun umbrella could trick the snow into not falling in the winter. It was just that this bride was not very good at telling lies with her face, and her expressions confessed every secret that her heart would have had her hide from the whole world if she could. The secret of sadness.

Nidra explained... "Maybe she was sad about something, or sad about many different things, or perhaps she was just sad. To me there isn't anything peculiar or strange about being sad on any day, even if there is no apparent reason. Sadness doesn't recognise weddings, or holidays, or weekends. It won't forget to be there on the day a child is born, or on the day you become very rich. It's a shadow that can follow you on any given day it chooses. It can follow brides, grooms and priests, from font to altar to grave. Bride is a title, wedding is a day, and days and titles change quickly. People and feelings change also, but not by the turn of a clock or the breaking of a calendar window. And that is why a bride who does not smile isn't strange; she is just human, just sad, just hurting."

And at the moment she finished speaking, a single tear trailed along Nidra's face as the lioness inside her fell back to rest after defending the good name of the beautiful bride, Nisudra. The other girls dropped their heads in shame and wept, for all of them at one time or another had known what it is like to carry a sadness inside of their hearts that they wished to keep secret from the whole world; because they were only human, too.

Albie's story *20th August 2017*

People tell me their stories; I don't know why, they just do. I suppose this story is written to try to replace a piece of jewellery that was lost a long time ago by somebody I care about.

Albie was the father of my friend, Danielle. Recently, she told me a story about a day she spent with him that she will never forget. It was at Christmastime when Danielle was only eleven. It had, by then, been two years since her mother and Albie's wife, Lesley, had passed away – leaving Albie to try and fulfil the role of both parents. Danielle and Albie were walking through Liverpool city centre, with its twinkling Christmas lights glistening like stars in the early evening sky. They were just passing through the side-alley that rolls from Lord Street down into the river of cobblestone that precedes the Bluecoat Chambers – she described to me how the wind ran mischievously cold and bitter that night, but carried Christmas magic with it. As she recounted this, I too remembered being a child and feeling those crisp, magical Lord Street winds cutting through me; those winds that ferry the cold from the docklands to become laced with the scent of onions from jumbo hot dog stalls. Those winds that portage the intermittent croaking cries of "EcKO!" from the old paper seller, then taxi his voice all the way up to the skeleton of a bombed-out church. Danielle described to me how in that side-street, on that day, in one of the side-door alcoves, sat a young lady. She said she could remember how cold the young lady looked; her coat was thin, offering very little protection from the cutting wind that seemed to be biting into her small, thin frame as they approached her. On the floor just outside the doorway where the young lady was sat, cross-legged on a piece of cardboard, they saw she had laid down her shawl; and on the shawl she had placed some quite crudely made wire jewellery.

Albie stopped to talk to the young lady, and asked where she was from. It transpired that she was a student from out of town, who was just nineteen years of age. Albie, seeing that the young girl was pretty much broke and just looking to make a few pounds to get by with, turned to Danielle, winked, and then asked her if the items for sale may make good Christmas presents for the family. Danielle, eager to help the young jewellery seller also, smiled back at her father and exclaimed, "Yes Dad, they'd make lovely presents!" Danielle perused the pieces of jewellery one by one, picking out her favourites, as the young makeshift merchant (quite cautiously, being grateful of any small sale) told Albie the prices of each piece in turn. Then, all of a sudden, to the shock of both girls, he softly asked, "Can I take all of them please, everything you have made?" The young lady covered her mouth in disbelief, and before she could even start to work out a price, Albie had reached into his pocket, peeled off some bank notes – with a value obviously far exceeding that of the jewellery in front of them all – and asked, "Will this do?" Filling up with tears, the student asked Albie if he was sure, and he kindly nodded 'yes'. Her hands were shaking as she gently took the money from his warm, kind hands.

Sale completed, the jewellery maker wrapped her shawl around her neck again, and Danielle and Albie held hands and started to make the journey home with full and happy hearts. Danielle said that she would never ever forget the smile on that young girl's face, and as she and her Albie walked away, they heard a shout from a hundred yards away – "Merry Christmas, and God bless you!" She didn't look cold anymore.

Danielle didn't ever see that jewellery again after that day; I guess that the jewellery was never important to Albie, and he may have just disposed of it in some way. I like to think that sort of thing may have happened often with Albie; perhaps often making gestures that were compassionately priceless, perhaps always looking for beautiful ways to help people out when he could. Telling me this story, Danielle said that she wished that she still had a piece of that jewellery, just to remember that day with him; because that was the day that she was proudest to be his daughter; the day she got to see just how big his heart was; the day he showed kindness and warmth to a stranger in a cold, Liverpool side-street.

This story is very special to Danielle, so I hope I've done both her and Albie justice in re-telling it; particularly as that was the last Christmas that Danielle and Albie spent together. Albie got his wings the following April – they say he never got over losing Lesley; that he died of a broken heart. With a heart so big, I truly believe that this may be true.

I am a story-teller – and I say that with the greatest of modesty, because I'm aware that I come from a whole city of story-tellers, born of an ancestry of story-telling. In Liverpool, there are story-tellers in all of our families; in all of our pubs, workplaces and on every street corner. This story is very special for me though, because it reminds me that for every story-teller, there are at least a dozen 'story-makers' where we live, with hearts as wide as the Mersey. They write their stories upon our side-streets and pavements with their actions and generosity; they sign their titles upon children's memories. They don't die until we forget them, and this is a way of honouring a true Liverpool story-maker; my way of keeping him alive in some way, for Danielle. Maybe it's just me, but personally I need to hear these stories; to feel inspired and proud of people, because times can be dark and can sometimes feel hopeless. Life is often overwhelming, and these stories bring me sanctuary and respite from it. They point me towards the type of person that I'd like to be; the type of story that I would like to write for my children, with my actions, and the type of memories that I would like to leave behind for the people I love. I have to hear them to remind me that; in the city where I live, if heart was measured in inches, some of us – like Albie – would be taller than the Liver birds.

In Memory of Albert Cook, 1955-1995.
Danielle, Summer, Angel, Juliet & Stanley send their love to you.

Shithouse culture *26th August 2017*

I suppose I'm growing up a little. I was out last night in the Swan pub in town. Outside, this great big fella had this other fella by the back of the neck, pushing his face into his and threatening him. My best friend is staring at the two, and commenting on how he hates bullies. I opted to not give it too much head space and change the subject, because I know it'll piss me off too, and the two seem to know each other. Then, the big fella starts slapping the little fella, and the little fella looks like he's about to start crying, and isn't even making an effort to stop himself from being slapped because he's too scared. So, my best friend is looking at me like 'are you gonna drop the big fella or is it my turn?' And I'm thinking that this is going to end really badly for this big guy if my friend hits him. So, I put my drink down and manage to get myself in between the two, and just say to the big guy, really nicely, "You need to stop hitting him now mate." He looks at me and my friend, then quickly weighs his options up, (and in a tremendous feat of street wisdom) decides that it is time to stop slapping the little fella. Anyway, we all walk back in the pub and the two lads seem to be friends again and are hugging each other and everything is sweet. Not saying this to look like a hero, because I'm far from it. This is just leading me to what I want to write about…

My friend said that he couldn't understand how a person could let somebody else slap them around like that, and a really interesting conversation started between us. My point of view on it was that some people haven't got the propensity to hit somebody, that – to me – is quite sweet, and I actually quite enjoy having people like that around me in my life. People who 'wouldn't hurt a fly'. I was raised in a 'shithouse culture' where if somebody wasn't a fighter, they were written off as a coward or a 'shithouse' (as we said back in the day). As I got older, I started to see things a little differently. I personally never liked fighting, but it was all part of my boyhood where I grew up. I was often sent out onto the field by my family to fight a bully when I was a kid. I'd generally be found hiding in the house because some older kid wanted to fight me and I didn't want to get beat up. "Get out there lad, or you'll be scared of him the rest of your life." They were right of course; one thing I learnt growing up was that being scared of getting a beating was much worse than getting a beating. It was more prolonged and involved more imagination of consequence. Thinking about it, that pretty much sums up what anxiety is; an 'imagination of consequence'. I can still remember sitting there on the couch watching *Brookside* in between my Nan and Granddad in their armchairs, sporting a bag of frozen peas pushed over a throbbing thick lip and one eye closing up after my pummelling. I'd be like a book on the shelf of that couch, ensconced between their bookend armchairs; perhaps a battered pre-pubescent personification of Lau Tzu's *The Art of War* with all of my most important pages misread and misunderstood (until much later in life). It didn't really matter if you'd lost, won or drawn to the family. What mattered was that you'd stood your ground and took your bumps well, so you could then sit back and be proud of your bruised and battle-weary young self. It's one of those tough love things that maybe only happens in working-class families. On the surface, it's brutal, but they are handing you life skills via a very clumsy, pugilistic rite of passage. A rite of passage that will one day enable and empower you to protect yourself and others, when you are alone and in-vitro, outside the protection of the family organism. As I said to my friend, "We were brought up with fists in our face, but not everyone was made to throw them back." Not everybody was brought up like we were, or gifted the same working-class, scuffed knuckled grit for homework. We were lucky in many ways, despite circumstantial adversity.

I think people are a lot like dogs, and some breeds just aren't made for fighting. But that 'shithouse culture' stigma that seems to deride them as a person is bullshit and through life experience of other people, I've learnt to let that go. You may get a guy who'd never throw a punch becoming a doctor and saving hundreds or thousands of lives over their career, or becoming a scientist that develops a cure for a disease. Perhaps a guy who becomes an IT expert that helps the police track down and arrest paedophiles, in doing so keeping children safe. I've known loads of men who 'wouldn't hurt a fly', great men, gentle people. To me, somebody being a bit handy with their fists isn't that much of a big deal. It's sort of one of those old ways of thinking that I've reflected on and changed.

That's what my friend and I talked about, as the bully and the little guy hugged it out at the bar.

Ice skaters & hugs *12th September 2017*

I wonder sometimes if we have an emotional memory as well as a cognitive one. I'm no expert in psychology, obviously, but people fascinate me sometimes. I saw my friend in the nursing home the other day; my fave, the lady on the dementia ward who keeps trying to escape. There was a part cordoned off as a building site that I was working on, and she kept sneaking in to talk to me. Every now and then a carer would come take her by the arm and escort her back. She'd sit there being good until they left, and then sneak back again to where I was, where she wasn't supposed to be, and we'd talk non-sensicles for a while as I threw cables across joists. They say she used to be an ice skater you know, world class. God, that's so easy to believe; some ladies just have a certain glamour about them, don't they. It's not a money thing – I'm guessing she's never really had money – it's a glamour thing. It's the way she holds her cigarette, the way she stands like a performer, the way she smiles like a dancer. I can spot a dancer a mile off just by the way they hold themselves, the way they walk; it's graceful. A dancer becomes the dance. I guess life is a dance in some ways, and we fall out of rhythm with it, and have to fall back in as we suffer the consequences of a missed step. Have you ever seen a dancer smile? They are taught it you know, it is beaten into them; if your hips are burning you smile. If your legs are falling off, smile! If Rico shoots Tony, you smile, because the show must go on! She has that same smile.

I digress (I do that a lot). The reason I mentioned emotional memory is this; when she sees me, she runs over for a hug, every time. Now it's never happened before, but this last time as she hugged me, she asked, "Who are you again?" I said, "I'm Ged the electrician," then she slapped my wrist gently and said, "I know that, silly," but we both knew that wasn't true and I feared perhaps she's deteriorating. I wondered how she knew I was a safe person to hug, but didn't actually really remember who I was. Maybe that's part of the condition, I don't know. But then I started thinking how, quite often, I meet somebody I've never met before and just get a feel of them; a familiarity or an aversion. Maybe it's an intuitive thing. I once read that we work on a number of different modes; instinct, intelligence and intuition. I think in many cases humans got so caught up their own intelligence that they fell below the beasts, became against what is natural, and lost their way to intuition and therefore consciousness. We became more important than nature and forgot that we are nature. Intuition is certainly emotional in many ways; a gut feeling, a hunch, a bad feel, a knowing in your bones beyond what you could possibly know practically. A knowing that is felt, not thought. Einstein studied intuition; believed it was the way forward for mankind. He said: "The rational mind is a faithful servant and the intuitive mind is a divine gift, we have created a society that honours the servant and has forgotten the gift." I'd be happy to go along with Albert on that one, however he lost me on the $E=MC^2$ thingy-magingy.

I wondered if, as the mind deteriorates, we get a little closer to instinct and intuition, and can just concentrate on who's OK to hug and talk non-sensicles with on building sites. Quite a feat while rocking the shit out of being glamorous at the same time, I thought.

God bless Mrs S.

Shields & pride *16th September 2017*

I bumped into a friend today and he told me his story. I've always liked the guy; some people you just take to, don't you. He'd told me he'd had a bit of a breakdown at the end of last year, when his father passed away. As per usual there was a combination of other undesirable life events on the peripheries of this, coinciding with his loss. If there's one thing I know about life, it's that when the shit-storm arrives, it all happens at once. He told me that seventeen years ago, his sister had passed away, and he'd found himself in a very dark place; he couldn't remember three years of it through drink and drugs. During the process of sorting himself out and getting dry, he met with a counsellor who changed the way he viewed the world. At the end of his course of counselling, the counsellor sat him down to give him a talk. He said that there was nothing else he could tell, show or teach him and from here on out he was going to be on his own, but he wanted to give him a gift for his journey. When my friend asked what it was, the counsellor acted out picking up an imaginary object as though it was heavy and cumbersome and passed it to my friend, then, pretending to take it from him, my friend asked him what it was. The counsellor told him it was a shield; a shield for all of the stuff that life was going to throw at him, and it would protect him well. He said that life will throw all sorts of spears and arrows at him and this shield was designed to stop them, deflect them, and protect his heart from being pierced again. He'd still feel the bumps, but he was less likely to be fatally wounded as long as he had that shield, because he now knew who he was and how to stay on the right path. But there was a warning that came with the gift. The counsellor cautioned him on how nobody in this life has an impenetrable shield; yes, some are stronger than others, but every now and then life will throw a spear at you and your shield may splinter, and if that ever happens you will be wounded and possibly die. He told my friend that if this ever happens to him, it will be time to come back and see him, and he would then tell him what to do next.

Seventeen years on from receiving that shield, my friend was in that dark place again after losing his father and was even considering having a drink. It was as though everything around him had fallen apart. He summoned the courage to find the counsellor again, tracked his whereabouts down to a university in Liverpool where he was now lecturing, and made the call he hoped he'd never have to make. Now, men can't ask for help very well, especially with emotional stuff. For a lot of us it's hard enough to stop and ask for driving directions, and there's a really good reason for that. As a man you are expected to know what you are doing, where you are going, and what life is all about. Truth is though, that we don't always know what we are doing and where we are going, and I haven't met a man yet who knows what life is all about. So, when we get lost, be that geographically, emotionally or spiritually, we are often too proud to ask for help. When my friend made the call to the counsellor, he didn't have to admit that he was lost or hurting or even ask for help, they already had a code in place. He just had to say "My shield is broken".

They met up and walked around a park for an hour and a half, and my friend expressed how he was feeling and opened his heart to the counsellor. He spoke about his hate, his anger, his bitterness, his hurt, and by the end of the walk his heart and throat were cleansed of the poison inside of him. He then asked the counsellor what he should do next about his broken shield. The counsellor looked back at him and asked him four questions.

"Do you know that this is your final journey?"

"Yes."

"And where does this journey end?"

"With my father and my sister."

"And are you ready to go with them now."

"No."

"And do you want to go with them tomorrow?"

"No."

My friend started to cry, and as he lifted his head, he received another gift.

"Then take this new shield and live."

The Stockies *17th September 2017*

Things were different when we were younger; apples came in all different shapes and sizes, the rain felt wetter and, well, 'rainier'. We grew up in Kirkby, bottom-end of Northwood facing Kirkby Town Football Club. Or as we called it 'The Stockies'. One theory was that it was once a venue for stock car racing and the name had stuck ever since. To be honest, we didn't ever check the origin of the name, to us it was unquestionably just 'The Stockies'. The Stockies basically consisted of a nightclub forming a bridge in between a circle of hills, and in the middle of that circle was a moat of concrete with a football pitch at its centre. Huge floodlights adorned the inner circumference of the hills that sloped towards the football pitch. Older boys used to 'borrow' the fire hoses from the high-rise flats, scale the floodlight scaffolds, then tie one end to the top in order to create a swing. The fact that you were swinging from a hill meant that you could run down the hill as you embarked on a swing outwards to pick up momentum, then swing off over the football pitches through a semi-circle of air and land back on the hill on t'other side. Every one of us had earned a broken bone from the Stockies swings, because if you were to fall it was usually right into the depths of the concrete moat. Looking back, we were amazingly creative in making a dangerous thing even more dangerous. Obviously, there was the swinging-by-one-hand trick, the upside-down trick, the two-to-a-swing trick, as boys do. Quite often we would light a bonfire to swing over and toss aerosols onto it, to later explode in a makeshift game of fire-swinging Russian Roulette. We'd sometimes steal the empty beer barrels from the nightclub and try to pop one of them in the fire, but for whatever reason we didn't ever manage to blow one up. We were hoping for a bomb-like effect, and in all honesty, I still feel like we missed out on that one.

The Stockies were our playground and we were the urchins and vandals of its eco system. I learned to ride a bike there, picked blackberries there, had fights there, had my first kiss with a girl there. I broke my arm there, made barbeques out of bricks and sheets of corrugated iron there, took my first hiding off a copper there for throwing an apple at his windscreen, hit golf balls at the buses travelling up and down Simonswood Lane from up on the hills there, ripped school uniforms on the barbed-wire fences there, we looked at our first nudey books there. No reflection on my parents; they brought us up right, but if there was trouble to be had then my brother and I were the meat in its sandwich. We'd go there almost every night after school to play. On a Saturday we'd get up early and sneak out of the house to steal milk from doorsteps, then down as many bottles in one go as we could on the Stockies grassy hills until somebody vomited, and they were the loser. Then we'd play in the stolen cars that the older boys had left there from Friday night, often trying to get them started, but they'd usually been ragged around the football pitch until they had run out of petrol or had their engines blown up. On a Friday night sometimes, I'd look out of my bedroom window and see the night-time silhouettes of the car robber's friends playing audience to the 'jockeying' of Ford Escort Ghias from the Stockies hills, as the stolen cars raced around the football pitch. Our house was so close you could see the headlights, hear the screech of tyres and the straining of overworked engines about to explode. I swear it was magic as a child, and I so longed to be driving one of those cars or at least be on those hills watching with the older boys. Nefarious misadventure has a certain enticing glamour to young children, I guess.

Just behind the Stockies was Knowsley Industrial Estate, which we trespassed and prowled upon, climbing fences into its factories. One day we stole/rescued the Dobermann guard dog from the scrap yard and brought it home. When we got home, I left my younger brother standing outside with her and went in to the house first to explain to my mother how it was mistreated and how "they leave it outside all night!" so we had to keep it. My mother opened the door to see this huge brown bitch Dobermann growling at her with my young brother standing next to it, gleefully smiling. Seemed it was OK with children, but didn't really take to adults; my brother was delicately talked inside by my mother, and the door was slammed quickly on the new would-be family member. We cried all night because we couldn't have our new dog. As a child I often became upset at how children could suffer such injustices at the hands of cruel and heartless adults, who should really know better! Then there was that time when I was about eight, and the police brought us home along with our pet Labrador, Ben. We'd climbed inside an old disused diesel tank on the grounds of one of the factories. The owner must have heard us and called the police. I'll always remember just hanging out in the tank and hearing "Police, we know you are in there, come out!" and, like meerkats, we popped our heads out to find three police cars, two riot vans and a car park full of 'bizzies'. To be fair most of them put their truncheons away and started laughing when they saw how tiny we were, I think they were expecting more hardened factory burglars. They insisted on taking us home in the police car. On the way home, we threw in a bit of drama, in an effort to get a release at the top of our street and walk home like nothing had happened. My brother and I came up with a plan to tell the WPC that our parents beat us up really bad if we got into trouble, and we might get murdered if we came home in a police car. This was all a charade of bullshit of course, my mother was only little and couldn't hit very hard even when she could catch us; we were fast and slippery as newts in olive oil. I suppose if that happened today, because of our fictitious plea bargaining there would be a call to social services and our parents would be arrested for child abuse, but things were a lot different thirty years ago. Poor Ben was wagging his tail in the back of the police car wondering what was going on; I guess that was just another day in the life of Ben, with being an urchin's pet and all.

My Mum was straight out the door all worried when she saw the police car pull up outside. The WPC was kind, and asked our Mum not to be too harsh on us as we were only playing, but needed to keep off private property in future. My Mum looked really calm when talking to the police and even used her 'posh voice', the one that she only usually used for certain phone calls. Although that 'posh voice' went away as the door closed and the police left. It changed into a banshee shriek I'll never forget: "YOU'VE EVEN GOT THE BLOODY DOG ARRESTED!" We did that run we always did up the stairs. All kids of my generation know that run, it's more like a fly than a run actually. You fly up the stairs like a rocket and intermittently a hand or a foot would touch the odd piece of stair carpet, until your head crashed into the Artex wall at the top of the landing scraping off a load of forehead skin, before you'd proceed to tumble down the landing looking for a hiding place and hoping she gets to your brother first so he gets the brunt of it and not you. Quite often you would feel a swipe of claws at your ankles from your Mum trying to catch the arse-end of you. If you ever got an ankle caught on the stairs it would be like one of those scenes from a horror movie, where a pack of zombies catch some poor human and pull them backwards to be eaten alive. You'd obviously not forget to scream out and make it seem like you were getting scull-dragged a lot more severely than you actually were. We were lucky that time; as we heard her from upstairs, laughing on the phone to my Auntie a little while later while reciting the tale of our arrest, she saw the funny side that time and that's now a regular story at Christmas in the Thompson house on a leap year.

Anyways, I thought the Stockies were all gone until this summer, they had long since built the David Lloyd gym on the old site. I was in there with Buddy and he went missing; he was supposed to be in the play area, but I couldn't find him and started to get a bit panicky. I'd only turned my back to him for a second to order a coffee. I ran out of the back door and shouted his name. His voice echoed back from what seemed like miles away, so I ran past the outdoor tennis courts to the rear of the gym's grounds where his voice was coming from. I found him sliding down a hill that you can't see from the gym. Then I realised, it was part of the Stockies; the only existing tiny part of the place of my childhood, the last little part of a hill. Buddy had found my childhood playground and ditched the indoor play area for it. He was smiling sliding down the hill like my brother and I used to do. It was strange because it was like seeing myself, like stepping back in time thirty or so years.

He'd found my playground and my memories.

The devil & a dead cockatoo *7th October 2017*

Once again, I found myself playing Devil's Advocate tonight in conversation, literally. Angels and demons play a major part in all spiritual beliefs in one form or another, and then again, there is their transfer to the psychological, wherein they become a metaphor for the internal emotional and psychological states of mind. There's sometimes very little difference between a spiritual demon and a neurosis or psychosis studied in mental illnesses. Apart from the fact that one is considered by many as a matter of science and the other as a mere superstition. In modern day UK the mindset is pretty much predominantly Christian which installs those images of Archangel Michael standing over a trodden-down demon with his sword, reinforcing the notion of Lucifer as Evil and God as good. But that to me is a very closed mind-set imposed from an organised religion which has some major good points, but I fear that, in the end, most organised religions are in one way or another morally questionable in the way they conduct their affairs and collect wealth. I think we transfer too much of ourselves onto the spiritual realm; war is a human concept, good and evil are also human concepts dictated via a judgemental mind. I doubt very much legions of angels and demons are locked in a constant battle for our souls in a parallel dimension. I think at some point someone projected the more internal struggle we face onto them.

When I was a child, I had this invisible friend named Fred. Now, Fred was a fucker. Fred ran over the pet Cockatoo 'Spike' with the lawnmower in the living room and killed him, he wrote my name all over the wallpaper, there was no end to his shenanigans. Until one day, my mother was getting me ready for school and she said "Look how good Fred is, he's already got his uniform on" and I ditched Fred and told my Mum he wasn't real so I wouldn't have to get ready. "Fuck Fred" thought Ged! Often when I hear these religious zealots blaming 'The Evil One' for everything I think "Fuck me, haven't you realised that Fred's dead yet?" Because to me that's what it is in many cases; a projection of their own inability to take responsibility for their/our own humanity. My understanding of it is that Lucifer wasn't cast down to control man or punish, just to be a consequence to man's actions. The devil might hold the door open, but it's human feet that step into the room of desire. Free will prevails as an ontological foundation of theorem. What I'm stating here is sort of an inversion of Nietzsche's "Only when God is dead can man be free", except in this case "Only when Fred was dead did Ged become free" because he was forced to abandon a projected phantom and take responsibility for all pet bird fatalities from that day forward.

The Eastern concepts of karma, Saṃsāra and consequence are, to me, a lot more common sense. Buddhism by its very nature lends itself to physics via the concept of karma, cause and consequence, action and equal and opposite reaction, ripple effect, echo effect, butterfly effect, along with the quantum physics theories of energy networks connecting all sentience and non-sentience on a universal scale. Removing the judgement from it, and the human projection of a war between dark and light, it then just becomes part of the cosmos; part of the great tapestry. Where angels and demons don't so much battle, but continually meet at a border, forever touching, but never being in the same place. In the same way that air and earth perpetually meet one another at an invisible border; a border that we live on, in and in-between of. In the middle-ground we have something to place our feet upon and something to breath ('*as above so below*'), at the extremes we are offered the possibility of flight and fall; and juxtaposed, the opportunity of being buried and bogged-down.

I'm not saying there is a God/Devil or that there isn't; that's possibly subjective based on experience and personal belief. I'm just saying that the moment that you take Fred out the equation is the moment you have to become more conscious about how you are acting. Both paradoxically and quite ironically, often the atheists get angry at the God they don't believe in for all the bad in the world, and the believers blame the devil for all the bad in the world because they need a bad guy. To fight Lucifer's corner here, I've met a lot of humans who Lucifer may be really embarrassed of, because they were just looking for a bogeyman to blame, and didn't have the courage to be bad responsibly and accept all the Hell that they have created around them.

Anyways, I'm going to bed.

Rest in Peace, Spike.
(My bad, sorry.)

Fish Finger Head *8th October 2017*

I'm often asked by Buddy to explain things to him that I don't quite understand myself. Often, there are no real answers, other than telling him that it's better not to wonder why. Like today for example – something was bothering him deeply, and he asked me a question about it that I couldn't answer; I could only advise him that, in life, you'll maybe never know.

For context, we were in a restaurant a couple of weeks ago, and on the next table to us sat an older lady with two children (about the same age as Buddy) who I would presume to be her grandchildren.

During the course of our meal, Buddy had noticed a disparity between our two tables; a gross and profound injustice, and a discrepancy in the space/time continuum that could possibly end the world if not resolved. To myself, the fact that the other children had colouring books and crayons and Buddy did not, was of course, of far less gravity – but I could see clearly that to Buddy this was a matter of unprecedented importance. As a parent you learn to negotiate as if it's a hostage situation; you must remain calm while dealing with radical forces that are Hell bent on achieving their goals. I wanted Buddy to finish his meal, but I also knew that there was a really good chance of him 'losing his shit' all over this restaurant if he wasn't appeased in some way. During what was quite an emotional debate from Buddy's side, I somehow managed to broker an agreement with him that if he finished his meal ("ALL OF IT?!" – "Yes Buddy, all of it!") he would be allowed to visit their table and ask 'politely' if he may join the other children in their artistic endeavours. To give him his due, as unhappy as he was with the outcome of the negotiations, he angrily and reluctantly accepted the terms. He began to quickly force down his meal gannet-style, while giving me the evil eye of enmity. Struggling to make some small act of contrition, I told him that he wouldn't have to eat his beans. Someone once said that there are two types of parents; 'good' ones and 'popular' ones. I was making a vain attempt at pulling something of the latter back.

Determined, angry and perspiring, he pushes the last of his meal into his cake-hole and departs our table happier; but still harbouring a smidge of distain for his miserable, killjoy father who had delayed his duties to art. He approaches their table, and in his most polite and hopeful voice, asks the lady sitting with the children, "Can I help them colour in as well please?" Now, I'm a great believer in the philosophy that you should never expect a 'yes' to a request, and that you should never have to apologise for saying 'no'. We have to careful not to expect too much from people for their, and our own, sakes. But there are certain ways of saying 'no', especially to children. So, when the lady looked Buddy up and down as if he was something that she had just trodden in, and told him that he would have to "Go away" with a dismissive and condescending backhanded shoo of her wrist, I thought (to use a word fashioned by my good friend Trisha) that she was being a bit of a 'twunt'. Now, being aware of the pre-eminent, infant fulmination that could potentially occur here, and also savvy to the fact that Buddy is neither aware of the delicate strategies involved in gracious retreat following a friend rejection, or good at being told 'no' to colouring in, I tentatively asked Buddy to return to our table.

Buddy just stood there, alone, at the foot of an inhospitable and uninhabitable alien table, looking heartbroken. "But why?" he asked. He's really gregarious; says 'hello' to everyone, asks questions, engages. He can't get his head around adults that don't like kids, particularly adults who don't like him (as rare as they are), because he's just trying to say hello and make friends. So, when the mean 'Hyacinth Bucket' ersatz of a lady again answers Buddy's "But Why?" by telling him that he must go back to his own table and "Leave us alone!" (with yet another dismissive and condescending backhanded shoo of her wrist) I thought I better intervene quickly. I walk over, take him by the hand and gently say, "Come on mate, you can't colour in with these kids, I'll get you some colouring in stuff on the way home." I just felt really sad for him. I pulled on his hand, but he didn't move; he was in a stare out with Hyacinth, and his heartbreak was rapidly being replaced by a fervent rage. His feet stuck to the floor like magnets; his eyes locked upon her dark soul, willing her back to the Hell she must have been born from so he could liberate colouring book Heaven from her tyranny. Hyacinth was staring back at him, laser beaming contempt towards this facetious, insolent child that 'should' know his place. After the longest five second staring dual ever, Hyacinth downed retina swords first, to see myself looking at her in complete bemusement, then turned her head away with a 'tut' of antipathy for us both.

Buddy's hand, gripped my own tightly. "Oh shite" I thought. It had started; I've witnessed the Budapocalypse many times before and this was in an uncontrolled social setting. I was half-tempted to make the sign of the cross, because I knew what was coming. I pulled on his arm to move him away, but he was – at that time – seemingly stronger than me. Hyacinth looked back at me in pompous scorn and disdain, almost smirking at this seemingly impotent father, unable to instil discipline enough to control the behaviour of a tiny child. I tried to drag him, but (maybe because of the rift in the space/time continuum that was occurring) he was too heavy! In anticipation of the explosion, I clutched him by the waist with both hands and heaved him up from behind by his hips, lifting his entire body from the floor. His head height was now matching my own. He then (bent double at his folding point, where I held him by the waist) lunged his entire upper body towards Hyacinth's table, while at the same time letting out a blood-curdling battle cry of "NOOOOOOOOOOOOOOOOOOOOOOOO!"

This was very unfortunate for Hyacinth, because due to Buddy's earlier speed-eating exploits, it quickly became apparent that he was still carrying within his mouth a cargo of semi-masticated fish fingers. So, at the point that Buddy screamed out, Hyacinth was inadvertently pelted with a hail of fish fingers embalmed in saliva. Perhaps even some of Buddy's breakfast was in with it, given the volume and profound velocity of the guttural outburst. Admittedly, I did find it rather amusing as I watched those little bits of fish finger and spit ricocheting off her head, and then struggled not to laugh as I watched her wipe off the pieces that had stuck to her with exaggerated serviette gestures of complete disgust. To give her some commendation, she wiped herself down with a degree of dignity – given the culinary assault she had just been subjected to by Buds – but she missed a big piece of fish finger at the top of her hair, so maybe she could have done with getting to a mirror quite soon-ish. I hope she saw my shoulders blades bouncing up and down in chuckle fits as I grappled with and man-handled my cute little, drooling, snot-dripping, tearful mess of an angel back to our own table, kicking and screaming. I didn't see 'poetic justice' on the restaurant menu that day, but my little guy was certainly serving it in bucket-loads at Hyacinth's table.

That was a couple of weeks ago – but going back to where I started this story, it must have played on Buddy's mind, because today he asked me "Why didn't that woman want to speak to me?" At first, I didn't know what he was talking about; Buddy always thinks you know exactly what subject he has in mind because he's thinking of it and gets terribly annoyed with you when you don't. He looked a little upset though, so I talked it out with him, to get to the bottom of what was bothering him.

"What woman Son?"

"The woman who wouldn't say hello."

"When?"

"The other day!"

"Where?"

"When she didn't like me."

(This went on for a bit until he said) "The woman I spat the fish fingers on when I kicked off."

"Ohhhhhh fish finger head!"

"Ye Daddy, fish finger head!"

(Official nickname created at 13:50 Sunday 08/10/17)

"Oh, she just didn't like you."

"Why?"

"She just didn't, that's all."

"Is it just me she doesn't like?"

"Probably not, but that doesn't matter either."

"Why?"

"Because there will always be people who don't like you."

"Why?"

"There's loads of reasons, but you have to remember that it's not you, you're OK the way you are."

"Why didn't she like me then?"

(So I searched for my best 'Gedaphor' and asked him) "Do you like chocolate?"

"Ye, chocolate is nice."

"Well, some people don't like chocolate."

"Oh."

"But there's nothing wrong with the taste of chocolate is there?"

"No."

"Well, it's like that sometimes with people, they just don't like you, but there's nothing wrong with you, and not much you can do about that, it's just like that sometimes."

"OK Daddy."

Buddy then seemed more at ease with himself. I like that about metaphors; they make things easy to understand.

I suppose it's one of the things I've learnt as I've got older. In the past, like everybody else at one stage or another, I suppose, I've pondered why people are as they are. I've come up with a lot of different theories, mostly based around malcontent, bitterness, jealousy and prejudice. However, I worked out one day that sometimes the answer is changing the question; in this case, from *"Why don't they like me?"* to *"Do I like me?"*

I hope he gets it now; it'll save him a lot of wondering for no reason in the future.

Chair catchers *9th October 2017*

My friend gave me a meditation to do once. She said, "Imagine you are on a chair and all around of you are the people who are involved in your life just now. Then let each one stand behind you and tilt the chair back, just to its balancing point, and then let it fall backwards. See who catches it, and make your life choices based on that." I did it, and it was a very strange and bizarre experience. Some people did catch the chair and some people who were taking up a lot of time in my life didn't. In the meditation some people were chair catchers and some people weren't; one person smiled as I fell (as if gloating), which wasn't a surprise really. I saw another particular person appear in the meditation with no hands who was looking embarrassed. I understood that it meant that they would catch me if I fell, but just didn't have the tools to deal with looking after themselves, never mind anyone else.

Because he had a good heart and would if he could, I kept the chair catchers and the guy with no hands.

Black dogs & Bruce Springsteen *25th October 2017*

Sometimes I hear this little voice from inside telling me to do something and generally, if I listen to that voice (and that's a massive 'if') it's advantageous to me. Call it what you will; intuition, higher-self, etc, sometimes I listen to the voice and sometimes I don't. Anyways, I went into the outdoor pool the other night at the gym, and at a certain point the little voice said "You need to get out now", but I ignored it. With the result of that being that somebody locked the door behind me, and I was left in my wet shorts knocking on the window for fifteen minutes, shivering and thinking what a feckless idiot I was for not listening to the voice. Then when I got in the car, I was hooking my phone up to play some music and the same voice said "Put the radio on". I at that point considered it wise to put the radio on. It's a very curious, almost comical Pinocchio versus Jimmety Cricket affair that goes on inside of me sometimes. But such is life; we all know what we should be doing but are very rarely caught in the act of fulfilling that role. Anyways, I clicked the radio on, and on came an interview with Bruce Springsteen. Among other things, he was talking about his encounters with depression, and I could relate to pretty much everything he said. I'm just coming out of a bout that's lasted a few weeks, possibly more now, it can be hard to pinpoint where it starts and ends. It sort of creeps in like background music that you weren't really paying attention to whatsoever until the annoying song is stuck in your head and you can't stop humming to it. It's a strange phenomenon that is very hard to describe, and can be quite awful at times. It's a part of being me that I'm still learning about and has probably impacted on every relationship in my life. I believe we all have two primary relationships that the other relationships we involve ourselves with orbit around, these being our relationship with ourselves, and our relationship with the world around us. For me at least; depression sort of alters these primary two relationships making them inharmonious, which sends a ripple effect into the tertiary relationships that encompass our interactions and relationships with other people. (Fuck me, I almost convinced myself I knew what I was talking about there, but don't worry, I'm winging this write as always.)

I like to believe that no experience has to be wasted, and during this recent wrestling match with the black dog I decided to try some different strategies based on what I've learnt along the way. First thing I did was taking it seriously and treating it with the same respect you would any physical impairment. I took some time off work to find a little head-space and centre, I afforded myself the luxury of being 'down' based on the belief that I was important. Now, that may sound strange to say, but one of things about depression is that you don't feel important, everything else seems important, except you. I sat down and had a word with myself and told me that I was important and that this issue was important to deal with and not ignore. (If you ignore it too long, it's the equivalent of saying that you are too busy driving to stop for fuel.) Second thing I did was that I was more honest and open about it, which was quite liberating because I realised that I was no longer embarrassed about the condition. It's just a transient part of who I am, but it isn't 'what' I am. I think talking to people close to you helps you a little, but more so them, in the way they know where you are at. I've learnt I've often been perceived as cold, distant or uncaring during a down period. It's sort of like when you are in a taxi and you forget to give the driver directions, because you presume that because you know where you are going, he will too. In the same way you presume that the taxi driver knows where you are going, you also presume that other people will know that your change in behaviour is nothing to do with them; rather just something going on inside you. But I've come to realise that they often don't, and that's not their fault, it's because I haven't ever explained it. Recently explaining it to two of the people closest to me, one of them being my best friend and the other my oldest Son, I realised how masterfully I'd concealed it, as surprisingly, neither of them knew it was an issue to me. I just always presumed they knew and they'd always presumed that there was nothing to know.

I think Bruce Springsteen really helped me. At points in the interview it felt like he was giving me a little pep talk. I thought to myself, "If Bruce can have depression, so can fucking I." In fact, Bruce didn't just talk about depression, he rocked the shit out of depression and made it look as rock and roll as an amp with a dial that goes up to eleven instead of ten. I also felt this huge admiration for him too; I thought this is a guy who really knows himself and has sought help from himself and others to learn the ins and outs of this condition. He was quite clear that without his condition, he never would have written all those songs or be the artist and person that he is today. And I guess when you can appreciate that, it's not such a bad thing after all.

Thankfully I'm on my way back up from this down spell now, there's no overnight or magic cure, but loads of things that do really help; meditation, yoga, writing, walking in nature, etc. But this time is a bit different, I've learnt a little more, and people around me have learnt a little more because I've been more open, I've de-stigmatised the condition with myself and accepted it fully.

Best of all, I'm coming back up like a fucking rock star.

Don't fear the Reaper *18th November 2017*

The breakfast in bed discussion with Buddy this morning revolved around the difference between Dementors from the Harry Potter film and the Grim Reaper.

At one point he asks me…

"Dad, does the Grim Reaper bite you?"

"No Son."

"What does he do then?"

"Well, there's a little string called an ethereal chord that ties us to the world we live in, and when it's time for us to leave he comes and cuts that chord for us so we can move on to whatever is next. You know, like when Granddad Brian died and he went to be an angel."

"So, he's not a baddy then is he?!"

"No Son, not if you look at it like that, he's nothing to be scared of."

Buddy smiles.

Truth is that I don't know if this is true, but if it is a lie then it's one of the most beautiful lies I have.

Finding home in Knoydart *20th November 2017*

I suppose it's very possible to fall in love with a place; in fact, I know now that it is perfectly possible to do so. A couple of years ago I embarked on a walking expedition from Fort William to a place called Knoydart, with the aim being to visit the most remote pub in the British Isles, The Old Forge. Being on a peninsular, Knoydart is only accessible via ferry or foot. I had gone in search of a pint, but upon arriving found so much more. Knoydart is a jewel in the crown of the Scottish wilderness, a place where myriads of stars speckle the evening sky, and the sand (due to its high mica content) glistens as the wind creates mini whirlwinds on its beaches, like sand genies manifesting from a magical lamp. Deer and stag roam freely on its hills, and embedded in the roots of overturned trees lay large chunks of crystal. The longer I stayed there I found myself growing more and more enamoured with its simple charm and most of all, its quiet. At the heart of every rock, grain of sand and tree, seems to exist a sentience of meditative silence. Even early on, it became very clear to me that I had at last found my spiritual home. On the walker's path in, we were greeted with landscape views of sea, sky and rolling hills of amber green with an almost tangible auric field of purple haze. We drank directly from crystal clear mountain streams and waterfalls as we watched this masterpiece of nature unfold before us. Tesla once said "My brain is only a receiver, in the universe there is a core from which we obtain knowledge, strength and inspiration." If this is true, I felt that I had stumbled across one of the core's greatest secrets when I found my place in Knoydart. I visit as often as possible now, as if returning to a geographical concubine imparting her serenity upon the spirit of man. There are no street lights, no police, no sirens, no evidences at all of any need for such things. Car keys are left in ignitions and no door is ever locked, or traveller made to feel unwelcome. The sociological philosophies of the village's inhabitants are built upon a bedrock of trust and mutual respect, the likes of which I have never witnessed as a city-dweller. I had unwittingly arrived as a casualty of dystopia to stand witness to a utopian dream.

The old saying that "Nothing can cure the soul but the senses, just as nothing can cure the senses but the soul" became just a little bit truer to me.

Last breaths *29th November 2017*

There's like those moments isn't there? All moments are fleeting, but some moments are just huge. I was in the nursing home yesterday, and my friend who manages a part of it says to me "I know it's not your job, but can you look at this bed for me, the woman is dying and I can't sit the bed up, it's just broken…" So, I go in. The poor lady is there struggling for breath, and I'm always really aware of my physicality and the fact that I don't wear a staff uniform. I wouldn't want her to come around and see this big scary guy that she's unfamiliar with rooting around under her bed and scare her in any way. So even though her eyes are closed, I start talking to her, "I'm Ged the electrician, I've just come to fix the bed, I won't disturb you for long" etc. Then she opens her eyes, sees me, she starts trying to form words, and I move a little closer to try to hear her. It must have took everything in her to get the words out; she breathed in and out, in and out, lifted her head –"thank" – then in and out, in and out, in and out again – "you" – then fell back like she'd just completed a marathon. Just for a moment, time stood still; it was really overwhelming. You see, she didn't have many breaths left in her life, and she used some of them to apply gratitude to me. I felt really honoured as a human being in the way that she'd do that. It has sort of haunted me; not in a bad way, but in a lovely sort of way. Things do haunt me sometimes until I write about them, it's maybe the only way I can process them properly. Anyway, some moments are huge, and sad – yes – but also lovely.

The gods write their plays in paradox, I suppose.

When a leaf becomes a leave *11th December 2017*

I was at the nursing home today and Mrs S tried to escape again through a door I had left ajar as I was loading my tools into the van. I enticed her back towards the building with a cigarette, linking her arm and shepherding her back up the ramp towards the porch where she could smoke it while taking retreat from the wind. They aren't allowed to smoke there and she loved it when I told her that, but said I wouldn't tell on her to 'the guards' (as she jokingly calls them) because we were friends. We watched a leaf dance on the wind in front of us both and I asked her about being an ice skater and where her favourite places to visit had been. She couldn't remember, she just said, "I've been everywhere and done everything." She knows that without remembering, I know she does. As the trees swayed and that leaf danced, I felt somewhere deep inside of me that this will be Mrs S's last Christmas with us. She'll never know how two entries in the new book are all about how ballsy and glamorous I find her. How a ninety year old woman with dementia, who can't even remember my name anymore, inspires me to write so beautifully; in a way that I feel as if it's not even me writing it. We took a selfie picture together (she'd never had one), I want to remember her when she goes. I'll maybe only show it to a couple of people. God, I feel like the Grim Reaper writing this, but I know she's getting ready to move on, the leaf showed me that. Maybe she is getting ready to make her greatest escape yet, into the cosmos of angels. I'm a great believer that sometimes we are allowed to look into the soul of the universe and see things before they occur. It can be through dreaming, the fall of a card, or the dance of a leaf; no matter which we just know. I had to ring the doorbell to get her back in as the porch has no key code entry. One of the carers answered and started asking her why she'd been outside, a little agitated and concerned that she had escaped again. I walked her into the sitting room to get warm. I told them all that it was OK, that I'd taken her to the Grafton to go dancing and we were back now with no need to worry. Mrs S said thank you to me and I told her I'd pick her up next Friday to go dancing again. She smiled that glamorous smile, I think she was proud that everybody thought that a young man had taken her dancing, or maybe she believed she had been. I'm a little melancholy and sad tonight, I guess there are some leaves you never really want to see blown away, and you just wish they could dance in front of you forever. Maybe she has three entries in the new book now.

Maybe I'll end this here, with a dancing leaf.

NB: The Grafton was a famous and popular Liverpool nightclub fondly remembered by people of her generation, and later generations to come.

Just one more thing...

One of the things that I'm proudest of is that I don't have to look too far to find a hero. I'm blessed to be in the position that my two greatest sources of inspiration in this life are my two Sons. I know of very few people who have been through so much adversity in their lives and come out of it on the other side as amazing human beings. My youngest, Buddy, who has suffered two heart attacks, a stroke and the resulting major brain damage, but still managed to attend main stream school and lead a relatively extraordinary life, and my oldest, James. James had his hopes of being an Olympian and of a military career crushed in a velodrome accident; he suffered a major head injury and was, for some time, paralysed. Since then he has achieved things which I couldn't possibly; he has shown everybody around him that with the right amount of motivation and self-belief, we can achieve almost anything we put our hearts and minds to. The next piece is an article I wrote for an online magazine some time ago. Or maybe James wrote it; I always like to think that life and its participants write the stories. Writers such as I merely trace around its and their outlines with words.

Anyways, this is maybe my favourite true life fairytale...

On his own two feet *22nd October 2016*

It was around 8pm on the 18th of September 2016. It was dark, the air was damp and I was walking the streets of Tenby, South Wales, resisting the urge to cry my heart out in the middle of a street full of strangers I would probably never see again. Although admittedly ridiculous, I sometimes wonder if the hardest fight most of the tough men of my generation and before will ever experience is the fight to never cry in front of another living soul. What made it harder not to burst into tears was that my mind was spinning – it had just cast me back around two years, to about the time of the accident.

My eldest Son, James, had blossomed into quite an athlete and cycling was his life – winning numerous races and already being scouted by the Olympic talent squad, it seemed there was no stopping him. Then, one evening, a near-fatal racing accident involving him suffering a massive head trauma brought that story to a very abrupt full stop. James was kept in a coma for a long time whilst the swelling and bleeding on his brain was monitored, and as a family all we could do was wait for him to come around. When he did open his eyes, physically and mentally he wasn't the same lad that had got on his bike to race that day, as the brain injury had caused a huge amount of damage. He had lost all use of the right side of his body and left side usage was limited. Cognitively he had restricted awareness and could only communicate to us through confused vocal grunts and eye movements. We didn't know how much he would improve.

As I walked past the arches in the centre of Tenby town, my mind cast back to how he was at that time. We were unsure how much James was aware of, as regards the severity of his injuries, or if he could even remember the accident.

There was one thing I knew though, that he knew that he wasn't right. He recognised me, but looked away when I made eye contact with him, as though he was embarrassed of the way he was in front of me. I got that totally, he was a young man, fit and strong several weeks ago and now he was almost paralysed, not only unable to do the simplest things for himself, but with the added frustration of not being able to ask for anything either. The day he couldn't hold my gaze I felt my heart break for him and to make it worse, there was nothing I could say or do to help him. It was one of the saddest moments of my life.

One day I got my chance to do something for him. In a way which I thought at the time was hauntingly like a scene from the film about Christy Brown's life, *My Left Foot*, James was kicking his left foot into the air to draw attention to the fact that he required help whilst also doing his best to tell me something. He was calling out and pointing his eyes to the corner of the room. I had become quite acquainted with James' dialect of gruntinese, but was initially struggling to understand what he was saying. It soon became clear that he was gesturing towards the toilet in the corner of the room and needed to go. I said I'd call a nurse, but the left foot almost hit the ceiling and a grunt resembling "Fuck that!" became decipherable. James had a plan; he was walking for a shit on his own two feet. He wasn't going to be hoisted or craned or wheeled there by nurses anymore, he was going to be shitting on his own terms, but he just needed a little help from somebody who was reckless enough to help him break the hospital rules and make that plan happen. I looked at him and said, "We are going to get in so much trouble if we do this, are you sure?" Now, to do it I would have to disconnect his inflatable leg thingies that stopped him getting blood clots while bed-bound, his NG tube that fed him, and his monitoring equipment.

He looked at me and grunted "Ye" and I saw hope in his eyes for the first time in a long time, I knew he needed a small victory or his spirit may break. There's an old saying which claims that in every moment of our lives we all have one foot in a fairytale and the other in an abyss. I've experienced this to be true and I believe that the only thing that can give us a light for navigating that abyss is hope, and James was looking for some hope. Going against all things sensible, practical and medical, I disconnected the tubes etc, lifted him to his feet, propped him on my shoulder, and James started to shuffle. He began a 4 metre marathon. Using me as a prop for his weight, he stepped a few inches at a time with his left foot and then dragged his right foot behind him all the way to the toilet and then back again. When he got back to the bed he was exhausted, but smiling like I hadn't seen him smile in a very, very long time. He'd taken a very small part of his everyday life back, but not just that, a little bit of his independence, pride and hope had been restored.

I obviously took a major ear-bashing over that one, but I'd make the same choice again – the heart does not understand logic and often pisses in the face of health and safety when need be. Where was I going with this? I digress, forgive me…

That's it… I was walking through Tenby too tough to cry and remembering stuff from a couple of years ago that made it even harder not to cry. Since his accident a couple of years before, James had conquered more than getting to the toilet. He'd psychologically and physically rehabbed, found his way back to the gym, back to the swimming pool, back on this bike, back to full-time study, got a part-time job after school, ran a half marathon, a full marathon and a triathlon. He'd also somewhere along the way managed to earn me the title of Granddad (my recovery is still ongoing from that one, and may take longer than his), but he's become an amazing Dad to little Anna. His recovery was so inspiring that Lance

Armstrong actually flew him over to Texas to give a talk on overcoming adversity on behalf of the charity he officiates in the United States. Now Anna and the rest of his family were all in Tenby and everyone wanted to cry.

It had been a very long emotional day for us all, but especially James. On this day James had taken on the Tenby Iron Man Challenge. The Iron Man Triathlon consists of a 2.4 mile (3.9 kilometre) open water sea swim, a 112 mile (180 kilometre) bike ride and a 26.2 mile (42.1 kilometre) run. It was dreamt up by some pretty sadistic Navy Seals as a fitness challenge for the US military's physical elite and then later adapted to a triathlon, with the first being held in Hawaii in the late '70s. It's a major achievement to even finish it within its 17 hour cut-off time and is viewed by many athletes as the ultimate physical challenge. They say it's more of a feat of survival than a race, and the lad who had struggled to shuffle four meters to go for a shit on his own two feet was – at any time now – about to cross its finish line and start eating a pizza I'd been guarding for him. It seemed our James had shuffled from the abyss to the fairytale and had become a hope and inspiration to all of us during the course of it.

The strength of the human spirit is a remarkable thing. Victor Frankl stated that "Forces beyond your control can take away everything you possess except one thing, your freedom to choose how you will respond to the situation." James has never read any of Doctor Frankl's work, but proved his point via action. James completed the Tenby Iron Man in 13 hours 45 minutes, the same way that he shuffled for a shit, on his own two feet.

He didn't need my help anymore and I doubt now that he will have any trouble looking any man in the eye for the rest of his life.

Acknowledgements

I'd firstly like to thank everybody that trusted me enough to tell me their stories; on an emotional level, we are all just little bundles of hopes, dreams and fears.
I'm honoured that you would share with me all three.

A special thank you also to…

Katie Wrigley
for the logo

Elle Buetow
for the author photograph

Gerry Thompson
for late night proofreading

Ryan Leahey
for the introduction and invaluable editing advice

Holly Fowler
for the cover artwork and illustrations

Paul Neads
for the printing and publishing advice

About the Author

Ged Thompson lives in Liverpool, in a house with a monkey puzzle tree and a rabbit named Velveteen, who often eats his flowers. When he's not being an electrician, he works with children in schools and in social services care, delivering workshops based around mental health awareness and emotional expression via poetry and story composition. Sometimes he writes books like this one.

Author photo by Elle Buetow

Instagram: gedthompsonpoet
Twitter: gedthompsonpoet
Facebook: Ged Thompson Writer

Also from this Author

If you liked this, perhaps you should check out
Ged's previous book, *Middle Earth Magic*, a collection of
magical fairytales for adults and children alike.
Available from Amazon.

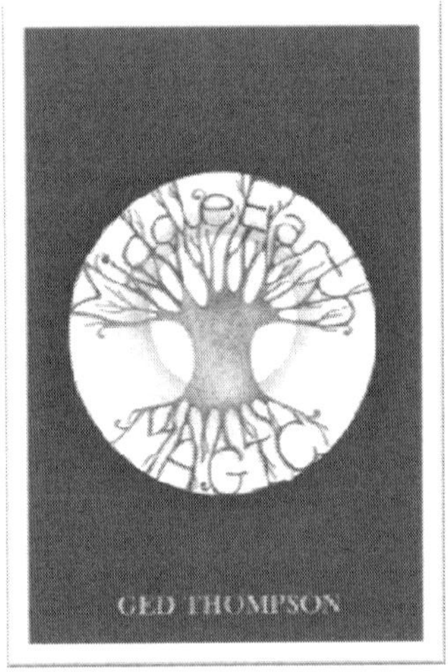

Workshops Available

Ged is currently designing and leading our educational poetry workshop projects. These projects aim to develop emotional and cognitive development via writing and performance-based poetry/storytelling.
If you would like to know more about the different ranges of art-based workshops we have available, please contact us on angeluspoetry@yahoo.com.